<u>Selma's Spirit</u>

A Story of Love and Forgiveness
A Journey to Peace

Sandy Thibault

Selma's Spirit
A Story of Love and Forgiveness
A Journey to Peace

By Sandy Thibault

All rights reserved.
Copyright 2004 by Sandy Thibault
Cover art copyright 2004 by Sandy Thibault
First Printing - September 2004
Second Printing - February 2010

GRAPHIC DESIGN BY SHERI CLARK

LIBRARY OF CONGRESS CATALOGING – IN– PUBLICATION DATA

ISBN 978-0-9759236-0-3

1. Self-Help   2.Abuse   3.Spirituality

Author Contact:
Sandy Thibault
InnerLight Healing Center
www.counselingandhealing.com
inpeaceandjoy@msn.com

Printed at:
Cornerstone Copy Center
20200 Heritage Drive • Lakeville, MN 55044
13775 Frontier Court • Burnsville, MN 55337
www.cornerstonecopy.com

10 9 8 7 6 5 4 3 2 1 0

This book is dedicated to Selma Amanda Bartsch.

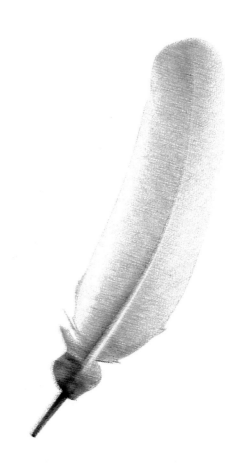

ACKNOWLEDGEMENTS

An endeavor of this magnitude is never a solo journey. I would like to acknowledge with my deepest gratitude:

To my patient and wonderful husband Jerry, who continually supported me even when I was impossible to live with. You saw the importance of this book and never allowed me to give up.

To my sons, Brent, Chris and Matt, who showed great courage as I told my story. They supported and encouraged me even when I sat at the computer and cried.

To my friends who loved and supported me, first as I made peace with my past and then through the writing of this book. You did everything from wiping the tears from my eyes to reading the manuscript and encouraged me to keep on writing.

To Jane Sisler, who planted the seed in me to write the book. She then nurtured it continuously with love and encouragement.

To Muriel, who helped me do the healing work that I thought was impossible to do. I am grateful for your love and compassion.

To Ken Olson, who was the first one to read the book. He was also my first editor, spending countless hours reading and editing several revisions. I am deeply grateful for his undying love and support during the writing of this book.

To Ms. Dale Wolf, who gave me a precious gift of professionally editing the manuscript. Her generosity and kindness was greatly appreciated.

To my brothers, Royce, Curt and Duane, for being supportive of my need to tell this story.

A gift is not always recognized as such. It is in its full embrace, that the real gift becomes visible. - Sandy Thibault

If one advances confidently in the direction of his dreams

And endeavors to live the life which he has imagined,

He will meet with a success unexpected in common hours.

-*Henry David Thoreau*

Selma's Spirit

A Story of Love and Forgiveness

A Journey to Peace

By Sandy Thibault

In our time…

Imagine…

Fear will give way to love

Anger and violence will melt away

Just as the waves roll in and out of our lives

We will find the center of our own peace

And then like the wind

We will find our course and set our sails

Let the spirit carry us to places yet unknown

We will find the light inside fueled by the energy of oneness

that is

this world… past…present…future…

To be our authentic selves

Opening our hearts, acknowledging our truth

Allowing love to flow in and through us to every living thing

Imagine…

Sandy Thibault

PROLOGUE

I had never considered telling my story. In fact, quite the opposite was true. All my adult life I had gone to great lengths to be sure no one would ever find out the truth about me. To acknowledge what had happened in my life brought nothing but raw emotion and excruciating pain. I couldn't imagine what people would think of me if they really knew the circumstances of my childhood. My fear of being judged was too high a price to pay.

My husband and close friends knew I'd grown up in a "difficult situation," but I never allowed anyone to know all the details of my life or the depth of my pain. My brothers and I never talked about our childhood or the abuse we suffered. It brought them the same emotions and hurt that it did me. I had believed that there was no way to make peace with this incredible burden. The only thing I knew how to do was to keep hiding from the truth about my life. I had learned to do this very well. In fact, I had mastered it.

Sometimes we find ourselves in places in our lives that we did not choose or expect. It's as though new grand plans are unfolding and with them, opportunities for our own healing are placed in front of us. When I look back I can see evidence of this woven throughout my life. I am in awe of the divine guidance that was at work. This is especially true in the telling of this story.

It was one such set of circumstances that led me to tell my story.

Since I began sharing the horrible story of my life, many amazing experiences and opportunities have presented themselves to me as I've journeyed down the path to peace. The impact these events have had on my life has been incredible, completely changing my perception of who I am and my place in this world. I have created a new relationship with God, a relationship that I learned to nurture with love and compassion.

It is possible to see all the blessings life has to offer despite the pain that life may have brought you. There is great power that comes when you choose to look at your truth, acknowledge and accept it, and then let it go. What I have to say comes from my heart. It comes from the wisdom I have uncovered within myself. I have looked at the darkness and the light and through it all, have found the blessings in my life. This book is a story of hope, healing and inspiration. It is about my incredible journey to wholeness through healing body, mind and spirit. It is a journey of faith and about creating a new relationship with God.

Behind my story lies the message that you can learn to love yourself despite the pain that life has brought you. Every day I learn this lesson all over again. We have to go beyond the depths of our despair in order to find our strength and beauty. Beyond the fear and vulnerability we find our courage and see the goodness in our lives.

The Calling

*I have always known that
at last I would take this road,
but yesterday I did not know
it would be today.*

-Narihara

Introduction

As a child, I was fascinated with other people's lives. I wanted to know how and why people did the things they did. I was eager to learn as much as I could about other's lives and the things they valued, what motivated them, and what was important to them. I believed there was a secret meaning to life and if I learned everything I could about others, I'd discover the secret.

My search began when I was a child through reading. I was a very poor reader, but my Grandma Selma was determined to change that. She believed that any obstacle could be overcome with enough willpower and hard work, and she was certain that this would prove true with my reading ability as well. She was single-minded in her mission to ensure this would happen.

Our little town's library, a historic 1800's era building, sat on a corner just a block off Main Street. The lush, picturesque grounds offered a serene home fit for such a building. The grass was the perfect shade of green and the flowers were colorful and vibrant. The building, a reddish tan brick had large rounded windows that spanned its entire length. Though not particularly stately or inviting, it still seemed to speak to me. I was as fascinated by its exterior as I was by all the information contained within.

The inside of the library was a place of comfort and dreams, my personal refuge. The books told me what life was like for others and gave me a glimpse of a world that was much bigger than the one in which I lived. When I was here I could take myself away — both literally and figuratively — from what was happening in my own house and dream about what might one day be possible.

My dad often prevented Grandma Selma from seeing me. Selma, my mom's mother, knew all too well what was going on behind the closed doors of our house. Every chance she could, she went to great lengths to protect my brothers and me. For this my dad hated her.

A woman of purpose, Grandma Selma knew it was important to make the best use of the time we spent together. There were two places she would often take me. One was the library where we read and checked out books; the other was Woolworth's soda fountain for a soda or ice cream. Because grandma never got her driver's license, grandpa drove us. He was a willing chauffeur and always managed to find ways to occupy himself while grandma and I spent time together.

I loved sitting next to her at the soda fountain counter. I would sit as close to her as stools bolted to the floor would allow. I so loved to feel her presence beside me. She always wore a dress and looked very proper. It was important to look your best, she said, because you never knew who you might run into. And people always stopped by to talk to her. She had many friends and it was obvious that they admired and respected her. I wondered why she never introduced me as her granddaughter, but soon realized it was because her friends knew who I was. I had the feeling that they knew more about me and my family than I did.

I was proud to sit next to grandma and was always polite, not wanting to embarrass her or make her angry with me. Though I loved her very much and I knew how much she loved me, it was clear that she expected more of me than was normally expected of other children my age. I never questioned this; I just knew that was how it was.

I enjoyed every minute I spent with Grandma Selma. Naturally, I relished the treats she bought me, but more important was what she taught me about life, living and — right now — reading. When we'd approach the library, she'd hold my hand. I thought she did this because I was apprehensive about going to the library. Since I wasn't a good reader it was an intimidating place as much as it was a place of dreams. But what scared me more was that grandma expected me to become a good reader and I didn't want to disappoint her.

In hindsight I've realized that Grandma Selma held my hand through many of the scary places in my life. Her hand in mine was reassurance and comfort against all the anguish that life brought. Now I can see that everything that grandma did was about preparing me to be strong and courageous in life.

Sometimes at the grocery store she'd tell me to pick out a treat, but I couldn't; I was unaccustomed to feeling that anything I wanted was important. This was her point exactly. So even though it was hard for me, we would never leave the store until I had picked something. This was Grandma's *other* mission (besides making sure I learned to read): To teach me how to stand up for myself.

Once she divided a cookie into two pieces, one bigger and one smaller. She asked me to choose one, so I picked the small piece. "What makes you think you deserve the small half and not the bigger half?" she demanded. "You should fight for the things you want and never settle for less than that!"

My fascination with the lives and stories of other people led me to read biographies and autobiographies almost exclusively. I loved books about humanitarians — men and women who had devoted their lifetimes to causes that they believed would make the world a better place. Many of these people had overcome major obstacles and went on to give something back to the world, either by serving others or by giving hope and inspiration to others. I hoped that one day the same could be said of me.

I wanted to learn so much, I feared I might never satisfy my curiosity. My life was so different from that of other people that I felt like an outcast from society. Even at a young age,

I knew these stories had much to teach me about people and the world. Maybe in these stories I would find some words of inspiration and some hope to cling to.

As I got older, it was no longer possible to focus on the lives of other people. Though I never lost interest in the lives of other people, I had to put my fascination on the back burner as I struggled to get through each day and stay alive myself.

Other people's stories were no longer as important as acknowledging and accepting my own. My story is where I found the most important lessons. These were the lessons that taught me how to be fully present in the journey of my life, honor the past, and take ownership of it all.

My adult life has been good. I have what most people would find ideal: a loving husband, three wonderful sons, a nice home, and a comfortable income. My life is filled with family activities, job obligations, and many great relatives and friends. I live the American dream.

The only flaw was that there was a huge part of my past that I had chosen to overlook because it was too dreadful to acknowledge. I couldn't make peace with any part of it. But I had no idea what tremendous energy I was expending to suppress such intense emotions. A part of me was aware that someday I would have to face my past, but "someday" wasn't anytime soon.

For now my days were so busy playing the game of life that I didn't notice that that was all I was doing — playing. I was much too busy to realize that by not acknowledging my true past that the life I was living wasn't authentic. Actually I wouldn't have even known what that meant. It would never have been in my realm of thinking to realize that each time I chose to ignore my past I was choosing to live with hurt and anger; I was unable to see that I needed healing, much less see that healing was possible.

Somehow we believe that there is safety in hiding. And then, the very things from which we spend a lifetime hiding come a-knocking on our doors. Like uninvited guests, they come barreling in and don't leave until they're good and ready. They are everywhere we turn — an intrusive force, invading all aspects of our lives. And they aren't going anywhere until they're dealt with honestly and directly. One day my past showed up uninvited on my doorstep and demanded that I pay attention to it. The ghosts of my past were unwelcome, unavoidable and unbearable. They were asking too much of me.

Frightening and unfamiliar emotions came pouring out of me. My world was falling apart and I did not know how to help myself. Eating and sleeping were impossible. At work I only went through the motions, praying no one would ask me what was wrong. I used every ounce of my energy to keep my emotions at bay until I got home.

Making peace with my past was too painful to do. As I started this process of doing so I had no idea what was in store for me, but I also knew I could no longer tolerate my pain. My heart was aching so much that I thought it might literally break in two.

Until life deals us a blow that teaches us differently, we are accustomed to thinking that we can control things in such a way that they have predictable and acceptable outcomes. As I stood on the threshold of confronting my past, I wanted a promise that I would be okay — a promise that my world be right-side up again. But there were no promises, no magic kisses to make it all better. I would have to stop fighting control and put my trust in something much bigger than me.

The process of acknowledging my pain has been an incredible journey, but did not come without enormous risk. I went to places in my heart that I never thought I could go. I had to delve into the darkest places in my soul, and face my deepest fears, all in search of healing and wholeness.

Early in my life, the stories of others gave me hope for my own life. I never realized I had a story to tell, but as I acknowledged the truth of my physical, sexual and emotional abuse, my story took shape as a vehicle to help others. People wanted to know more, just like I had always wanted to know more about others. So, I decided to tell my story to offer hope and inspiration to others. It is my prayer that my story will awaken in you the amazing possibilities for healing and peace and will stir the spirit that lies deep within your heart. This story is my journey — a journey to find peace.

Chapter 1

Many of us have dates and events that have made permanent marks on our hearts and in our minds. I remember exactly where I was when I heard of President Kennedy's assassination and Princess Diana's death. More recent is the memory of the terrorist attacks of September 11, 2001. These kinds of events change our perceptions of the world and in turn, how we think and feel about life.

We all have personal events that hold great significance for us as well. There are many dates that are permanently etched in my heart. I recall the details like they happened yesterday; each memory brings up joy or sadness. My memories have a timeless quality to them.

April 11, 1999, is one of those dates. I had no idea how my life would be transformed by just one phone call. It's hard to imagine that one call would have the power to send my life into a tailspin.

It was an ordinary Sunday. We'd gone to church, as we always do, and then my family scattered in different directions. My husband and two of my sons went to the final tryouts for traveling baseball. Our whole family has been involved in baseball for many years, traveling to more than 40 games a year for each son. It was a way of life for us in the summer, but it was still pre-season so I still had a little time to myself. During this uninterrupted time I chose to clean the house. Though it was a job I dreaded, the reward of a clean house was worth the effort.

It always seems that as soon as you are really trying to get some work done, the phone won't stop ringing. And so it was on this day. After three phone interruptions, I decided to let the answering machine get any others. But since I happened to be walking by the phone when it rang again I decided to answer this one last call.

A male voice asked if he had reached Sandy Thibault. His voice was very familiar. My mind sorted through mental files so fast I think I created a breeze, but I still couldn't match the voice to any names. School? No. Church? No. Boy Scouts? Traveling sports? No and no. When he said, "This is a voice from your past," I instantly and with certainty knew who it was. There was dead silence; I was speechless. I felt a huge pressure in my chest and a deep, indescribable sadness in my heart. My knees went weak and I thought I might get sick.

The person on the other end of the phone was someone I had not spoken to in nearly 30 years. We had met when I was 14 and he was 20. His sister Barb and I were best friends in high school.

Ashamed of my family situation, I usually stayed to myself. I had nothing in common with the other girls, but for some reason Barb and I became close friends and I confided in her. Concerned about my home life, Barb shared our conversations with her older brother Tom, who began calling me and eventually asked me out.

I was very mature for a 14-year-old and flattered that I had been asked on a date, my first. As excited as I was, I was very embarrassed about my home. We lived in a house that had been considered unlivable and abandoned. Most of the people in our small town knew that we were poor and abused. It was no secret that we were poverty-stricken, but I thought I was successful at hiding the rest, though now I know that was not the case.

None of this mattered to Tom. He wasn't afraid of my father. In fact he came to our house and asked my father if he could date me. It's hard to imagine that any parent would allow their 14-year-old daughter to date a 20-year-old, but my dad did.

Tom's dad was the county sheriff. With all that went on in our house, I thought that this would have frightened my dad, but it did not. He firmly believed that what he did in his house was his business and he could treat his family as he chose.

Tom stayed by me during the violence that filled my life during the coming years. Sometimes he would pick me up for a date after I had just been beaten. He would find a place to park and hold me in his arms as I sobbed. Tom was tall and strong and when he put his arms around me I felt more secure than I knew I had a right to feel. Though I believed there was something very bad about me that made my own father treat me this way, right then I enjoyed Tom's comfort.

As hard as my life was then, the days ahead would be even worse. Tom stuck by me through them all. Without his support I would have killed myself, I'm sure of it. We had been together for six years and Tom had promised to marry me and always take care of me. I believed that we would always be together, so it was impossible for me to understand why he abruptly ended our relationship. I never heard from him again, until now — this quiet Sunday afternoon 30 years later.

Now here I was in my kitchen barely able to stand, unable to speak. My mind was flooded with questions that I couldn't voice: Why are you calling me? How did you find me? Why did you leave me? Whatever he had to say, I wasn't prepared for it.

As he began to speak I could hear that he was crying. I knew his words were heartfelt. "I have been looking for you for a very long time," he began, "I always knew that I would have to find you." He took a breath. "Not a day has gone by that I don't pray that God has kept you safe and helped you deal with your pain."

"God once allowed me to take care of you and now he has led me back to you," Tom went on. And then he acknowledged the reason for his call. "I have called to ask for your forgiveness. I promised you that we would get married and that I'd always take care of you."

Now at long last I learned why he'd suddenly disappeared from my life. "My parents disapproved of your family and forbade me to marry you. I should have fought for you; you were the love of my life. I've been married twice; each time I knew it should have been you I married. I've loved you and held you in my heart, all these years."

Though I could barely comprehend what he was saying, it felt like there had been no passage of time since we last talked. The 30 years disappeared and I was transported to a place and time I hadn't visited in a long, long time. I fought for composure in order to respond.

"I never understood what happened, but I didn't blame you," I shakily responded. "It had been literally pounded into me that I was unlovable, and your leaving me just affirmed that feeling."

What I said next was what he'd been hoping to hear. "I forgive you and I never stopped loving you. Nothing will ever take the place I have for you in my heart." These words came out of my mouth as though they were always there, waiting to be spoken. It was the truth. But it was also true that both of us were married now with families and different lives. My devastation over his broken promise was 30 years ago. During the intervening years I have never regretted that we were not married, but to tell him now would only hurt him more. I'd gone on to create a happy life for myself.

I thought he was finished but he was not. "Once I found you, I could have written you a letter but I needed to hear your voice and find out for myself how you are," he continued. "The way you grew up, I couldn't imagine how you'd be okay."

Tom had his own questions. Have you forgiven your parents for what they did to you? Have you forgiven Bud for raping you? He strongly felt that was something that I would have to do, if I hadn't already done so. "Anger and hatred will only destroy your spirit," he stated.

I could only sob; the emotions I had hid for so long were now visible. The protective walls I had built came tumbling down. In the rubble, the smoke and dust clouded my thinking. I stood in the middle of it all, vulnerable and naked, completely exposed.

Chapter 2

The sound of the back door slamming and the excited voices of my family startled me back to reality. Obviously tryouts had gone well. The event that had taken place during my family's absence felt like an episode of the Twilight Zone. I had suddenly been transported to another time and place, full of anger, violence and sorrow. It was now foreign and out of place. The chasm between these two worlds was enormous. How could this other life fit into my life now?

My response was automatic; I would hide this from my family just as I had hidden everything else that had been unpleasant. This was my only choice — there were no other options. No one would ever see how out of control my emotions were. To do otherwise meant I would have to let myself be vulnerable. I couldn't allow that to happen.

The following days were excruciatingly long. It was hard to tell the days from the nights. Because I couldn't sleep they were one long continuum. I couldn't eat; I functioned at the bare minimum. I cried uncontrollably on and off.

I lived a double life. It took considerable energy, not just to maintain a front for family and friends, but to also pretend to myself that things weren't spiraling out of control. I had buried my past 30 years before and I was intent on keeping it buried.

Tom's words replayed over and over in my head. Despite the fact that I had told him I forgave him, I could not help but feel anger for his abandonment. And how dare he call me now and demand that I forgive those that had abused me? What gave him this right? Didn't he understand what this would do to me? If he cared so much, why did he intrude now?

I needed my questions answered. After all, he was the one who had initiated this. He had given me his phone number at the end of our phone call and I used it now.

I'm sure he could sense my nervousness as I spoke. I wasn't interested in small talk; I wanted to know why he had called. We may daydream about looking up an old friend or lover but usually the thought remains only a daydream. What motivated him to call me?

Tom expressed his tremendous guilt over leaving me the way he did. "I loved you so much," he explained, "yet I didn't have the strength to fight my family for you. But I knew then that I would spend every day regretting what I did."

"I let you down when you needed me to help you get over the horrible things that happened to you," Tom lamented. "I needed to ask for your forgiveness."

I asked Tom if his wife knew that he had contacted me. "My wife has always known about you. She has always known how much I loved you and that I would find you and she understood. She's a very understanding woman."

"Are you thinking that we can be friends?" I asked.

"We are both married, have families and are committed to these relationships but I would like very much to have a friendship with you," he replied.

"I'm not sure I want or can have a friendship with you," I countered. "Knowing the relationship that we had, it would be too easy to cross the line. I don't think either of us wants to put our marriages or families at risk."

Tom agreed. As much as he wanted to pursue a friendship with me, it was possible that he'd want more. And hurting my family would be hurting me and this is something he wouldn't do. "Tom, why did you ask me if I have forgiven the people that hurt me?"

"I know that God put me in your life then to help you and keep you safe." Tom went on to explain that shortly after he'd disappeared from my life he had answered God's summons and become a healer. It became his conviction that he was on this earth to bring healing to people.

"You have always been in my heart and now is the time for you to heal and find peace," Tom explained. "If we choose, we can hear and feel His presence and call inside us. Sandy, this is your calling to heal and find peace and I am the messenger." He professed that he had prayed for me every day for the last 30 years and would continue to do so as I searched for peace. "I loved you so much that I was willing to ask you the hard questions."

The phone call that I thought would answer my questions only produced more. Was he crazy, I wondered? What was he talking about? He was speaking a foreign language that I didn't comprehend, yet at the same time I heard the truth in his words.

In the midst of my numbness and confusion, the ache that I felt hearing Tom's voice for the first time in so many years was still there. It felt like a foreign emotion then, but I now know it was the same ache that had been present throughout my childhood. It was the same ache I had when my dad screamed and told me how worthless I was. It was the same ache I felt when he backed up his words by beating them into me until he was exhausted. Suddenly and uncontrollably it all came back.

As much as I thought I was successfully masking my out-of-control emotions, I could not hide how I looked. No amount of make-up could hide the anguish on my face or the sadness in my eyes. I looked as if I'd lost my best friend, and in a way, I had.

Someone had died; that someone was me. I had compromised my soul by trading the privilege of knowing who I was for the illusion of safety. No additional words or explanations were necessary; I knew the price had been too high. I had denied myself peace.

Though I was a bit skeptical of Tom's mission and his

motivation, I also viewed his call as an opportunity to finally find healing and wholeness. At the time I was clueless about what healing and wholeness actually meant, but I was about to find out.

My wrung out appearance and obvious distress led me to confide in an acquaintance. Jane was a co-worker at school; we also attended the same church. I didn't know much about her, but knew intuitively that she was kindhearted and understanding. She could see I was struggling with something difficult and was respectful of my need for privacy. All I was capable of telling her was that I was dealing with some serious issues from my distant past. Jane understood that I needed help and suggested I start with our church pastor, Pastor Will.

In desperation, I went to see Pastor Will that very afternoon. Somehow he made sense out of what I said through my sobs. The dam broke and I told him the entire story of my childhood — the story that I had never told anyone in 30 years. He was a sympathetic and supportive listener. As much as he would have liked to be the one to provide me with counsel, he knew I needed a professional with more expertise. He strongly urged me to seek help from a therapist. When I left his office I knew I had just a few days to make an appointment, because Pastor Will would be checking back with me. He had helped me sort things out, but I still needed help to regain control…though it now occurred to me that being in control is just as much an illusion as selling your soul for safety is.

After my meeting with Pastor Will, Jane offered to listen

and help me any way she could. She had just been through an extremely difficult time in her own life, so I knew instinctively that she was someone who would understand. Several weeks later I was able to tell her my story. She listened as I told her all of it and responded with sincerity and wisdom. Little did either of us know that this was the beginning of a friendship that would sustain both of us through many of our lifes' struggles.

In my mind I had two choices, but my heart knew there was only one. Though I didn't know what "listening to your heart" really meant, I knew that its message was too strong to ignore. Unconsciously I knew that pretending my past had never happened was not an option. Hiding it all away again was impossible too.

My life had been like a new shirt wrapped in nice packaging. An outer covering protects the shirt. Under that there is more protection inside. Several pins and carefully placed cardboard insure that it remains neatly folded. But once that shirt is torn from its packaging, it's impossible to put it back the way it was. I had very carefully packaged myself in a wrapper — I looked elegant, neat and together. Further protection was in place to be sure that the various pieces of me would stay tucked inside.

Now my story and all its pieces were no longer safely tucked away. The hiding was over.

Between the anger and sadness, the fear was bigger than life itself. I was afraid of everything. I had only questions for which I thought there would never be any answers:

How deep was my sadness?

Would I ever stop crying?

Did I deserve to find peace?

How could I deal with the anger I felt toward Tom for opening this wound?

How could I let go of the anger at my dad for robbing me of my childhood?

How could I forgive the man who raped me over and over again?

How could I forgive my mom for not intervening?

What if I really was unlovable like my dad had taught me?

How could I learn to truly love and let myself be loved?

Could I forgive myself?

My life became a blur. Powerful emotions and feelings ran rampant throughout me. I didn't understand then how the body, mind and spirit all work in tandem. In my bewildered state of mind peace felt like a hopeless illusion.

Inside I was dying, yet I still had to move forward. I gathered up all the energy I could muster and with the help of Jane I made an appointment with a therapist she had recommended. I couldn't even will my hand to complete the paperwork; I could only nod in answer to the questions the receptionist asked. As I waited to see the therapist, both my head and heart were pounding fiercely, each at a different rhythm. Tears fell down my face at a steady pace, my stomach was knotted up and I felt like there was poison running through my veins. As Muriel, my therapist, introduced herself and led me to her office, I was sure I was about to vomit or pass out.

For the second time in recent weeks, I told my story. I told Muriel how I grew up in extreme poverty, how my brothers and I were taken from our parents due to abuse and neglect. I told her how my father verbally attacked me, and how he beat and kicked me until I was black and blue. I told her how my dad tried to kill us, and how I left home just after I turned 15. I told her how I had been raped over and over again in a home where I should have been safe. I told it all.

When I raised my head to look at her, Muriel's soft brown eyes were welled with tears. "Oh dear God," she said softly. We sat in silence, as we both absorbed all that had been both spoken and unspoken. It was then that I knew I was not sitting with just a therapist. In those moments I experienced the presence of real grace: acceptance and unconditional love for who I had been, who I was now, and who I would become, all encompassed by God's love. This was Muriel's gift to me, one that I could not give myself. Throughout my coming journey Muriel would teach me about unconditional love for myself and others, forgiveness, and the presence of God.

More than anything else I wanted peace and healing. In a quiet voice Muriel asked me, "Do you know what peace is?"

"No," I replied, "not really."

"Peace is the acknowledgement and the acceptance of your

truth. It's telling your truth without emotion. Peace is honoring your pain and letting it go. It's about unconditional love."

"I can't imagine what that would be like," I replied. "That's okay because I can believe it for you," Muriel responded. "I know you will find peace even if you cannot imagine it right now." She would hold a vision of peace for me as I worked through my pain.

The power to find peace, as it turns out, is in making an intention to do so with my heart. This was the beginning of my journey to peace, forgiveness, and unconditional love.

Shortly after my first visit with Muriel I found two beautiful small stones. One was periwinkle blue and inscribed with the word *imagine*. Surrounding the word was iridescent stars and half moons. The other stone said *believe* and was a frosted, opaque white. I carried the *imagine* stone in my pocket for almost a year and a half. The other stone I gave to Muriel who would help me believe in the things I could not yet imagine.

Unearthing something that had been hidden for so long was an arduous process. As my grief, loss, sadness and anger continued to surface, it was even harder to control the emotions that were emerging with the telling of the story. Yet I still had no idea how much was buried within my body, mind and spirit.

Just as Tom had said, to let my pain go I would first have to acknowledge the truth of what had happened to me. I'd never told anyone the complete story — not my closest friends and not my husband. I'd revealed bits and pieces here and there, but only when it was absolutely necessary.

I expected to be judged for what had happened to me. All through my childhood I felt I had been criticized for my families' situation by my peers and most adults I came in contact with. It could be seen in their actions or lack of actions. I believed this would still be true.

My dad repeatedly told me how bad I was and that our family problems were my fault. What if in making peace with my past I found out my father was right all along?

There was a great deal of shame in living the way I had. There was shame in being so obviously not cared for, shame in trying to hide the bruises, shame in being raped repeatedly, and shame in always being the focus of gossip in our community.

The thought of telling my story overwhelmed me. Many times I wished this story were someone else's, not mine. Unfortunately I could not simply wish away the pain; I had to acknowledge my past and make peace with it.

Muriel was a compassionate listener who continually reminded me that we were engaged in a sacred task as we uncovered each piece of my past. She taught me that this kind of healing is difficult to do alone and should be done in community with another person for guidance and support. As I started own the road, I would have to learn to trust Muriel with the deepest part of my soul in order to hopefully find the peace I so desperately wanted. Muriel believed I could find that peace and with her guidance, we set off on the journey.

Acknowledging the Truth

*In the middle of the journey of our life,
I came to myself within a dark wood
where the straight way was lost.*

- Dante

Chapter 3

Until I was about four, my parents and I lived in the apartment above my maternal grandparent's house. My mom worked as a nurse's aide at a local nursing home, a job she had trained for before she got married. Dad worked as a laborer for a small sign company. Most of the time I lived downstairs with Grandma and Grandpa. Mom and dad often went away for weekends and vacations and left me with my grandparents.

Grandma was used to caring for other people. When my Aunt Alice's parents died just months apart, she had cared for her. My Aunt Alice had a son my age named Jim. Jim was also left in grandma's care frequently as Alice struggled through life. Jim and I were as close as brother and sister during those early years and remained close throughout most of my childhood. Even now, separated by years, we share a special bond. Though too young to verbalize it, I think we both felt detached from our parents. Our grandparents loved us deeply, but there was still a feeling of loss. As I grew older and my family's life circumstances became even rockier, these stays with grandpa and grandma were the foundation that would sustain me.

When I was four, my parents and I moved to a rented house on the edge of town. The house was small and cozy. My grandparents were there all the time, so everything was right in my eyes. My dad hired a housekeeper named Beatrice, who also took care of me as well as the housework. Beatrice was affectionate and loving, giving me the love and cuddling that my own mom could not provide. She treated me as if I was her own daughter. Of course I was too young to understand my mother's mental health issues and how they affected her relationship with me, I just knew that I felt no connection to her. My mother figures were Beatrice and my grandma.

Soon after she came to work for us, Beatrice learned she had terminal cancer. Engaged at the time of her diagnosis, Beatrice went forward with her wedding, despite her grim prognosis. Her marriage resulted in a daughter, who was born a year before Beatrice died. About 20 years later I had the opportunity to met Beatrice's husband, George and daughter, Joy. George told me about my relationship with Beatrice and how much she'd loved me. Even though I'd been quite young and so many years had passed, I still feel a fondness for her. Perhaps she gave me the love she would never be able to give her own daughter.

We lived in our little house for less than a year when my dad lost his job at the sign company. Soon after, he started his own landscaping business. According to my relatives he didn't really know anything about landscaping or business, but according to my uncles, "he was too stubborn to let that stop him."

According to my grandma, my mom had a very difficult pregnancy with me and in fact, we both almost died during my birth. I was born six weeks prematurely and weighed less than five pounds. So fragile and guarded was my condition that I was baptized within minutes of being born.

I never really thrived as a baby and when I was five months old I became extremely ill. My parents and grandparents were told that if I lived, it would be nothing short of a miracle. Every year on my birthday, grandpa would tell me the story of the day they expected me to die. He had stopped at the hospital before work to see me just as the doctor was making his rounds. It was good that my grandpa had come when he had, the doctor said. I was so sick that he thought I would probably die that day. I can clearly picture grandpa sitting in his chair telling this story. By the time he finished he would have tears in his eyes and I would be feeling sorry for him. As I got older grandma told me I lived because "I had the will to live and through the grace of God."

When my father's abuse was at its worst, I would recall grandpa's story and I wished I *had* died. In my prayers, I asked God why he had not let me die and instead forced me to go through such hell. In my child's mind, dying would have been the best thing that could have happened to me. I wished it many times during my childhood. Somehow it just seemed easier.

I had never talked with my mom about the abuse, but about a year before she died I was able to ask her one question: "When did you know how violent dad was?"

"The minute you were born I could see the rage in his eyes," she responded. That was all she would say. Though I asked for more, she would give no explanation. We never talked about it again.

My brother Royce was born when I was five. His birth was also a difficult one, so harrowing that the doctor told my mom that her life was in danger if she had any more children. Mom didn't follow this advice; my brother Curt was born a few years later and my brother Duane followed almost exactly nine months after that.

When mom brought Royce home from the hospital, she was physically and emotionally exhausted and confined herself to her bed. She became disconnected from everything and everyone, though I was too young to understand it.

My grandma and great aunts came over every day when my dad left for work. They took care of all the household duties and almost always took off usually just before my dad came home.

It was about this time that I began to sense that my world was different than other people's worlds. I didn't know exactly how it was different, but I was aware it wasn't right. My dad had always had a short temper and got very angry at the slightest provocation, but it felt like overnight his anger became suddenly directed at me. I was his sweet little girl and then suddenly, I felt like he hated me.

When I began to talk about this in therapy, I was jarred by some disturbing memories. I remembered that my dad always wanted to be near me when we were alone. I remembered sitting on his lap, and his hand would be under my dress rubbing me. Many of these kinds of memories, though foggy, still haunted me. As I started to talk about them, I also did my best to deny them and push them away. With everything else I had endured, could he have sexually abused me as well? The knowledge of this was too much to bear.

Such memories distressed me even more because they were foggy. What else from my past did I not remember? Would a flood of memories just suddenly appear and terrorize me even more than I already was?

The power of the mind is amazing; Muriel taught me that it works in tandem with the spirit and will present what one needs at the right time. As hard as I tried to deny them, certain memories came up over and over again. I could feel their heaviness — a kind of grief — in every part of my body.

I knew then that my father had used my body for his pleasure and when it stopped I was no longer his little girl. He hated me. He hated how I looked, how I acted, and all the things I did, or failed to do. I could not be who he wanted me to be. Or perhaps he could not be who he wanted to be, so he would take his frustration out on me.

During the five years that we lived in that house, my whole

world changed. There were now four kids, I was 10, Royce was six, Curt four, and Duane three years old. My mom remained detached and uninvolved. My father continued to isolate us more and more. My grandmother and great aunts hadn't been allowed to come and help with the housework for a long time. I'd been fully responsible for the household duties for years; by the time I was eight I cooked and cleaned better than most adults. It was clear to me that my dad thought it was my responsibility to take my mom's place.

My dad didn't allow me to have any friends or do what other girls did…whatever that was. It didn't really matter; I didn't know how to make friends anyway. My world was so different from other girls my age, what would I have in common with them? Being isolated was much easier. In my limited free time my father allowed me to read or listen to the radio. When he did let me see my grandma, she would invite over her friends granddaughters so I could play with girls my age. Once I was even allowed to go on vacation with grandpa and grandma for a week. We went to a friend's house on a lake that had a granddaughter my age that I played with. The memory of that week of fun was something I clung to when times were bad.

My dad's temper was almost always accompanied by violence and we were never sure what would set him off. He was angry most of the time. He'd bring his face within inches of mine, and scream at me about how stupid and worthless I was. His face was red, veins bulged at his temples — a clear indication of how out of control he was — and I could see the fury burning in his eyes.

Besides being an angry man, he was extremely controlling. He had countless expectations that had to be met. He controlled everything, including the food we put in our mouths. He had very definite rules about what could be eaten and what could not. Treats and candy were not allowed without his okay, which meant they were few and far between.

This food restriction followed us everywhere, even to family birthday parties. We were given specific instructions about what we were allowed to eat, not eat and how to behave. While our cousins laughed and played we could only sit quietly and not draw any attention to ourselves. Still, I was always excited when we were allowed to attend these parties because I knew that there would be plenty of the kinds of food we were not permitted to have. The excitement was always short- lived; I knew if I was caught eating the forbidden food, I would pay the price in beatings, but I always had a spark of hope that maybe this time he would give in.

At one birthday party, my uncle carried around a tub filled with bottles of pop and let everyone choose the kind they wanted. When he got to me I told him I was not allowed to have any, but he assured me it was okay, after all this was a birthday celebration. Even though I knew better than to take one, I wanted so badly to have what everyone else had. As my hand reached for the icy cold bottle, my dad, who had been closely monitoring us, began to scream at me. I was humiliated and angry being yelled at in front of all my relatives attending the party. I found a place to hide in a back bedroom where my hurt came pouring out. My uncle found me and sat with me as I cried, and assured me that everything would be okay, but I knew better and so did he.

This control of our food became even worse as the years went on. We consistently had to prove that we'd worked hard enough to deserve to eat. Until then, I had no idea that food was considered a basic need. I thought it was something that had to be earned. In my world, everything was conditional.

The first time my dad beat me with his fist, I was eight. Many girls my age had short hair and were getting perms, and I wanted one too. Finally he let me get my long hair cut and to get the perm I so desperately wanted. But what I thought I wanted turned out awful — not at all like the other girls' perms. They looked cute and I looked ugly! I had hoped that if my hair looked like theirs, I could finally fit in.

In an effort to make it look better, I tried to brush it. My dad caught me and blew up; accusing me of ruining what he had just spent good money on. His response to me was instantaneous and violent. His fist hit my body with powerful blows that did not end until his rage was spent. I went to bed that night trying to comfort my body from the bruises he had inflicted.

From then on, every time he finished beating me he would yell, "I can't stand to look at you anymore, get the hell out of here!" I would then bury my head in my pillow, curl up in a ball and cry until I fell asleep. Crying released some of the emotion that was building up inside my body. Balled up in a fetal position gave me a feeling of security, at least for a few hours. But I knew when morning came, it would be another day of his terror.

I always tried to make sure that everything was perfect when my father got home from work, but that was no insurance against his temper. He was still uncomfortable with the strong connection I had to my grandma. Suspicious that I was telling her about his violent ways, he allowed me to spend even less time with her.

When my grandparents came to the house he made sure it was as uncomfortable as possible for them. He would verbally attack my grandmother whenever she would question him about how he had treated us. When he became angry at her, I would start to cry, which only made him angrier. Adding stress to what was already an unbearable situation, dad's business was failing and we had little money.

My mom had once again retreated to her bedroom; I hadn't seen her in weeks. Sometimes she would answer a question through the door so at least I knew she was in there. On the rare occasion I was let in, I would find her in bed with no plans of getting up in the immediate future. She usually asked me what I wanted, then asked me to leave and close the door behind me. I often sat at the end of her bed and begged her to get up for just a little while, but she always refused.

I was at a point where I could no longer see beyond my own needs. I wanted and needed a mom, I wanted to be loved and cared for. I wanted her to care about me and to be part of my life. At an early age I came to the conclusion that no child should come to: My parents did not love me. It would take many years and much healing to understand that they did love me but were not capable of showing their love. That still didn't make it hurt any less.

My grandma and my great aunts eventually told me more about my mother. She had a normal childhood but as she grew older they noticed that she had some personality quirks. As a teenager and young adult she was unable to make decisions for herself. They often wondered why it was so hard for her to get her life together. They worried that she would be unable to stand up for herself. This helped me understand why grandma thought this was an essential skill for me to learn.

We knew little about my dad's family and what was known was kept very quiet. Rumor had it that my dad's mother, Grandma Lily, had kicked her husband out when my dad and his sister were very young. She took back her maiden name and worked hard to make a living for the family. Much later we learned that this wasn't exactly the case. The truth was that Lily's husband had left her because she was so violent he could no longer tolerate living with her. I also learned that Lily often left my dad with her parents who beat him for every minor infraction. Now I have intimate knowledge of how the cycle of abuse continues.

Chapter 4

Whenever my dad got violently mad at grandma for trying to take care of us she would stay away for a while, so that her presence didn't provoke him even more. When things would settle down a bit, Grandma Selma and my great aunts would start to come again. They were careful to never arrive until after my dad went to work.

When I came home from school I would be so excited to see grandma, I would fall into her arms. She would hug me, hold me in her lap, and let me stay there wrapped in her arms for as long as I wanted. I felt safe and loved.

Grandma Selma was a woman ahead of her time. Self-actualized and aware, she understood the power of forgiveness and that anger and hate will destroy one's spirit. When I was eight or nine, grandma sat me down on the sofa and talked to me about God and about forgiving my dad for what he was doing. "God made him just like he made us," she said. I could not believe that. She told me that God would always be with me and love me. How could that be? If that were true, how could He let these things happen to me? Maybe God hated me too. What kind of God would let this hurt continue? If there was a God, He was definitely not there for me.

Now that grandma and her sisters were back caring for the house and us kids, I overheard bits and pieces of their conversations. Grandma told them that she had bailed my dad out of jail recently, after he was caught drinking with teenage girls at a nearby lake. The stress of dad's failing business and his violent ways were taking an even greater toll and grandma was worried about leaving us alone with him every night. My mom had not been out of bed at all for several months. Grandma said she'd had a nervous breakdown. I did not understand what this meant, but I knew it wasn't good.

Everything was an awful mess; how could it ever get better? I can remember grandma sitting at our kitchen table, sobbing, trying to figure out how to fix our horrible situation. Someone had to do something and grandma believed that it was her responsibility to do so.

One day, I returned from school and found grandma there as she usually was. Although she tried to act normal, I sensed something different about her and became scared. She hugged me and promised me that everything would be okay. Grandma always left before my dad got home but tonight grandpa joined her and they stayed for dinner. Dinner was completely silent.

When it was over we were sent to bed without having to do any work…clear indication that something was very wrong.

I huddled next to my closed door so I could hear the conversation coming from the living room. There was a loud argument between my dad and my grandparents. Though I don't remember now what the argument was about, I can only imagine what was said. The screaming went on for what seemed like several hours. Finally it got quieter and I could hear my dad rummaging through the closet…the closet where he kept his guns. My heart raced and I was close to hysterical. I had to stay silent when all I wanted to do was cry and scream.

When I heard them in the back yard, I looked out my window. I could see through the shadows that my dad had my grandparents backed up against the garage. He stood a distance from them with a gun pointed at them. "I'll kill you!" he screamed at them. Terrified, I had to turn away. I couldn't breathe.

What would happen to us if he killed them? As I inched back toward the window, I heard their car starting; they must have run for their lives. I could still hear dad screaming and saw him waving the gun wildly. I wondered what would happen next. If he came for me, what would he do to me? I curled my body into my usual ball and quietly sobbed. Through all of this, my mom was in bed. She was not able to help us. Dear God, someone please help us.

When I awoke in the morning, grandma was sitting next to me. She handed me a suitcase. "Pack as much as you can, as fast as you can and then get dressed," she said quietly. "When you're done packing you can go wait out front for grandpa." I was shaking in fear, but did as I was told. Grandpa had parked behind the house to stay out of sight; soon he drove around to the front of the house. After I was in the car, they loaded my mom in the back seat and we drove off.

Before waking me, grandma had gotten Curt and Duane up and sent them to her sister's for the day. Royce was already in school. I learned later that the school was notified about the situation and told to call the police if my dad came there looking for us.

In the car grandma explained to me that she would do everything in her power to keep us safe. Royce, Curt, Duane and I were going to stay with my grandparents for now. But this was bittersweet. As much as I loved to be at grandma's, I knew how dad would react when he discovered what she'd done and I knew that things would end up being worse for us. It seemed better to survive one day at a time than to endure the inevitable torture that would most certainly come our way in the end.

That day we drove to Rochester where my mom was committed to the State Hospital. I was sad and confused, on the ride back I got sick and my whole body ached. Though I was safe with my grandparents who proved they would risk their lives for me, I felt so empty inside.

Predictably when dad came home from work and discovered what had happened, he came to grandma's to get us back. But grandma, smart woman that she was, had the police waiting for him. Though it was never discussed, a restraining order may have been in place. While I could avoid watching the scene in the front yard, I was unable to shut out the terrifying sound of his anger. When the police came they eventually were able to calm him down.

My 10-year-old brain could not grasp this entire trauma, nor could my body and spirit. I began to unconsciously learn ways to cope with these events that I was too young to understand.

A month or so later, grandma told me that dad was coming to pick us up for an afternoon visit. She held me close and explained that this hurt her immensely, but she had to obey the court; she had no choice but to make us go. I was paralyzed with fear. Who would protect us? How could we be forced to spend time with the man that had abused me so horribly and threatened to kill the people who loved us most? I thought if I was sick I would not have to go, so I taught myself how to throw up as a way to get out of going with him. My stomach always hurt with emotional pain so doing this was also a small relief from the hurt. But as I said before, grandma was smart. I got away with this once, not twice.

Forced to obey the court order, grandma taught me what to do to protect my brothers and myself. She told me to never let them out of my sight, the four of us were to stay together and not be separated. She told me what to say to someone if I needed help. Grandma pinned a tiny envelope to the inside hem of my dress. It contained a small amount of money, her phone number and other emergency numbers.

Our visits with our father became progressively more violent as he interrogated me about my grandmother. She was emotionally poisoning me against him, he claimed. He hated her and talked about how he would kill her as soon as he got us out of there. I did my best to not react to what he said until I was alone in my room. There I could sob into my pillow over the hopelessness of our situation. Because he knew how much I loved her, he took out his anger toward her on me. He expressed pity for grandpa for being stuck with someone like grandma and never blamed him for anything.

Grandma's forgiving nature did not allow her to harbor the same anger. Before each visit, she would remind me that I would someday have to forgive my father for what he was doing. She always said to me, "If your father knew what he was doing to you, he could not live with himself. Remember he is still your father and you owe that to him." Owe him? I owed him forgiveness? Though I would never be disrespectful to grandma, I was too angry and hurt to think about forgiving him.

Conversations with grandma often took a spiritual turn as well. She was preparing me mentally and spiritually to cope with my circumstances. Grandma understood the damage that was being done and knew that there would be a time in my life when I would have to come to terms with it. Since it was unlikely that she would be there to help me, she was preparing me now. Neither of us knew the worst was still to come.

In the interest of self-preservation, I had learned to completely shut down. There were lapses in my memory about things that were just too painful to recall. It wasn't until I began unraveling my story that I realized how much I had blocked out. At first this disturbed me, but with Muriel's help, I learned that if it were important for me to remember, the memory would surface. Although Royce was much younger, he was able to fill in some of the blanks.

During the six months my mom was in Rochester's State Hospital, we lived with grandma and our lives took on a normal pattern. At least as normal as it could be when we did not know what was awaiting us around the next corner. By this time my dad had lost both the house and his business. He'd moved to St. Paul and was renting a house there. Royce recalls that my father had a girlfriend.

On one of our visits with my dad, we went to his house in St. Paul for the weekend. I was afraid of the big city because I didn't know how to keep us safe there. This constant insecurity weighed heavily on me. When we arrived at the house, there were many adults there who appeared to just be hanging around. When they asked me numerous questions about my dad, I understood that these were social workers who were there to assess our situation. If I told them the truth about my dad's anger I would be beaten, maybe even killed.

Trusting these strangers was too big of a risk to take; it was better to lie. I had to do what was best for my brothers and me; after all I was responsible for their safety.

After the social workers left I remember being so afraid of the city and afraid for our safety that I wanted to run away. Before I had a chance to act on this idea, there was screaming and fighting and the police and an ambulance came. The rest of the weekend's events are blurry for me, but Royce's memories are crystal clear. He remembers that mom was there, on a weekend pass from the hospital. Mom and dad had a fight and in an attempt to escape my dad, mom jumped out of a second floor window. Still fleeing, she severely injured her knee when next she tried to jump off a large retaining wall, in an attempt to kill herself. My only memory of that day is flashing lights and sirens.

Somehow we got back to grandma's after this traumatic event. But this marked the final brick in the wall I had been slowly building around myself that no one, not even grandma, would penetrate.

After a stay in the hospital to repair her knee, my mom went back to the State Hospital. My brothers and I were once again safe with grandma, but I knew it would not stay that way; it was just a matter of time until we would have to go back to live with dad.

It was several months later, when that day arrived. My mom was released from the hospital and all six of us moved into a house in a suburb of St. Paul. We lived in a neighborhood with kids our age and I began to think things might be better. I was still uneasy because, for the first time, I did not know how to contact my grandma who was more than an hour away from us.

This was no accident. Dad had us in hiding, keeping our where-abouts secret. But grandma was persistent and eventually — after several months — found us.

In a risky move, grandma sent me a letter. She took the chance that I would get to the mail before dad, which I almost always did. From then on it was our plan that I would always get the mail so that she would be able to send me letters without anyone knowing. She sent me stamps and told me where to go to mail the letters. She also taught me how to make a collect phone call. Even from a distance she was teaching me how to keep my brothers and me safe. I felt a small sense of victory that we had been able to defeat my dad's best laid plans. Albeit on a limited basis, I was in contact with my lifeline — the only person in the world who I knew loved us and wanted to protect us.

Because I was mature for my age and good with children, I became an in-demand babysitter. I took every babysitting job I could get, sometimes babysitting almost every night of the week. For the first time I had my own money. I used it for two things: clothes for me and my brothers and once a week I bought a cherry Coke for me and candy for my brothers. I knew these treats were dangerous; they were just another reason for my father to be angry, as though he needed another reason. But we were becoming experts at keeping secrets…from him, the world, and ultimately even from ourselves.

The rest of the money I kept hidden for the day when I would run away. Looking back at 12-year-old me, I'm amazed at the courage and intelligence I had then, knowing that my only way out was to run away. Yet even then, before I learned the art of visualization, I visualized a flame inside my heart, sometimes sensing it so strongly I could feel its warmth. That feeling came with knowledge that amidst the terror in my life, I would persevere and be able to help my brothers. I would help all of us create a better life than the one we were living. If I could survive, there would be a way out.

The hitting had let up a bit, but dad was still verbally abusive and out of control most of the time. He still would put his face within inches from mine and scream at me, though the rants varied. "You are evil just like your grandmother, and this was her fault," was his latest tirade. My dad felt that grandma hated him and was trying to turn us against him. As her accomplice, all this was my fault too, he raged. "What did I ever do to deserve this kind of treatment from you?"

"You will pay for what you've done!" His favorite tirade at me was "You're a no good son of a bitch. You are no good...nothing but trouble." These words were beaten into me and screamed at me most of my life. It's easy to see why I came to believe them. I still struggle everyday with my own sense of worth.

Certain that everything he said must be true, one night I decided that life for everyone would be easier without me. Yes, at the ripe old age of 12, I thought it would be better if I killed myself. Calmly and logically, I considered what to do and how to carry it out. I collected every pill I could find in the house and took them into my bedroom. I sat cross-legged on my bed and carefully laid the pills out in neat piles. I organized each pile by pill type, with a few unclassified tablets on the side. My room was clean and organized just like the pills laid out on the bed. Exactly the opposite of what my life was really like. I gazed at the pills, both prescription and non-prescription, not certain that I had enough to kill myself. Nor did I know how to get more or stronger pills. I did know that if I failed in this attempt, my dad would beat me so badly I would wish even more that I were dead. I was trapped; there was nothing I could do. I carefully put the pills away and life, if you could call it that, continued.

One day in June, just a few weeks before my 13th birthday, my dad left with my mother. Mom was sick again and of course, according to dad, it was all grandma's and my fault. Without telling us, he had taken mom to Hastings State Hospital and committed her for treatment. Though we had never known what it was like to have a real mom, it was still a loss to have her gone. He said he would also be gone for a while, and then he left. Later I found out that he had checked himself into the psychiatric unit of a St. Paul Hospital. It remains a mystery to me what prompted him to seek out help for himself at this particular time.

He'd hired Jack, a 20-year-old man to live with us and take care of us. Jack and his girlfriend Sarah were very nice to us. They cooked us delicious meals. They paid attention to us. They played with us and we were delighted by their company. Sarah taught me how to care for my nails and apply nail polish. We hadn't been this wonderfully cared for since we had been at grandma's.

Early one morning, just days before my 13th birthday, the doorbell rang. Standing at our door were policemen, social workers, and grandpa and grandma. The police carted Jack and Sarah away. An officer, the social workers, and grandpa and grandma remained behind with my brothers and me. It wasn't safe for us to stay with Jack, my grandparents explained; we were going back to live with them. Then grandma, the police officer and a social worker took me to my bedroom and shut the door. They asked me if Jack had touched me or hurt me in any way. I was naïve and not sure what they were implying. I said no, but they continued to question me. Where my dad found a person like Jack is beyond my comprehension.

The next day I was taken to the courthouse. There I met with various groups of people who I now know were psychologists, social workers and police officers. They explained that Jack had a history of sexually abusing girls and they suspected that he had hurt me as well. They pleaded with me to tell them what had happened so they could help me. Grandma cried and begged me to please tell them the truth.

I was telling the truth. Jack had not touched me. Years later, when I realized I had memory lapses, I would wonder if he had and that I had blocked it out. Now that I was learning to pay attention to my heart, my memories of this and my heart were in harmony. I knew he had not hurt me.

This was not the case with the memories of my father. They were definitely not in harmony with my heart. As much as I would like to have explained away my memories, my heart knew differently. One day while I was working on a speech about my life, something that I wrote triggered memories of what my dad had done to me. As these memories rushed in, for a while all I could do was cry. After I allowed the grief to pour out of me I was finally able to acknowledge the ugliness of what had happened. I knew my heart wouldn't lie.

After the "Jack" incident we went back to grandmas for several months and then back to the house in St. Paul with our parents. We were still surviving day to day, never knowing what was ahead for us. This hell was far from over.

Chapter 5

One night, in the dark of the night, dad moved us to a house out in the country near Lindstrom, Minnesota. We moved there in the late spring just before my 14th birthday. The house was a two-story with gray siding that resembled shingles. Waist-high weeds surrounded it. Most of its windows were broken out. The dilapidated porch, which sloped so much one could barely walk on it, spanned the entire front of the house which faced the lake. Weeds twisted up through the broken boards and crawled up the pillars.

The barn was across the road and in much better condition than the house, but still badly in need of paint and repair. The rest of the outbuildings looked like they might cave in with the slightest breeze. It was easy for me to imagine that in years gone by that this farm was well cared for. The property sat at the end of a road, and straight ahead was South Center Lake. At the end of the road another road wound around the lake, which was populated by summer cabins. The "summer" people drove past our house to get to their cabins.

We all worked night and day to make this place, which was not fit for humans to live in, habitable. We had running water that didn't run in the winter when it froze. The house had central heat that kept the main floor tolerably warm but not the upstairs which was bone-chillingly cold. The house was so poorly insulated that we could feel the wind blow right through the walls. Our attic was home to a large number of bats. In the warmth of summertime, the stench from their droppings was unbearable.

Again, unbeknownst to the rest of us, my dad had us in hiding. He planned to keep us as many steps as possible away from my grandma or anyone else who might take us away. I hadn't realized it would be possible, but after the loss of our last house, dad became even more violent. The reality of our situation must have finally hit him. My dad worked as a laborer but never made enough for us to live, much less fix up the house. Our situation was steadily getting worse and he must have felt like the world was caving in around him.

In this new place I again felt isolated and alone. In St. Paul we had close neighbors but this house was five miles from town and away from people. The only exceptions were on summer weekends when people came to their cabins. It should have been comforting that no one knew anything about us, but it wasn't. I was terrified because I didn't know who to turn to if

I needed help.

Our only saving grace was the horses. I'm not sure how we could afford them, but my dad always had them as long as I could remember. In fact, he had nice saddles and all the tack to go with it. When I was small he would train the horses and enter local horse shows. As we got older, my brothers and I could see that the horses were cared for better than we were. The barn was warmer in winter and they always had more than enough oats and hay to eat.

The families that drove by our house on the way to their cabins would sometimes stop to look at the horses. My brothers and I decided that we could offer horseback rides and charge for them. This was a way to make a little money and get to know the "summer" people. Their kids became our summer friends. We often exchanged horseback rides for rides on their speedboats. I became a great slalom water skier while we lived there. Having friends was a new experience for me and I found out I was good at it: I was elated by it.

These friendships were so important to me. The school we attended was quite small and most of the other kids had been classmates all of their lives. It was hard for us to be the new kids. It was made worse by our raggedy and unkempt appearance, which assured that we stood out from everyone else.

Like all of our fun times, our new friendships were only possible when my dad was at work. I worked twice as fast to get all the housework done before he came home, but it was worth every bit of effort. For the first time I had something to look forward to.

My dad's temper continued to rage most of the time, so the only time we had any peace was when he was at work. Life for us was always hard and, despite the horses, it became even harder at the farm. The house wasn't fit for barn animals much less a family with four children. Our situation was futile.

A few months before moving to Lindstrom, dad had checked mom out of Hastings State Hospital. At home she once again retreated to her bed, so it was up to me to take care of the household the best I could, which was never good enough for my father. It was extremely difficult because we had so little money. Many times we had no phone, electricity or oil to burn for heat. Food was scarce and hardly any of our clothing fit.

Despite these obstacles, my dad held me accountable for these things that were not in my control, like the food I put on the table or the clothes I should have been able to mend.

The horses were our refuge. Royce and I would get up as soon as my dad left for work, bridle the horses, jump on bareback, and go for long rides. How peaceful it was to ride next to the stream and into the woods, enjoy the beauty of nature, and forget about our lives for a little while. We knew that the horses felt our pain and loved us anyway. As the horses walked we became one with their motion and the rhythm of their hooves as they hit the ground. We got lost in this feeling. The horses were indeed a healing balm for our broken spirits.

Dad's verbal abuse and physical beatings were constant, and I was never prepared for what laid ahead. He started by yelling and screaming and ramped up when I did not have responses to his accusations or when I was unable to obey his commands. The beatings began with his clenched fist usually by punching me in my upper arms and in the middle of my back. When I turned away to protect myself he became even more vicious, kicking me in the back and grabbing my hair. My hair was long and he would wind it around his fist a couple of times and pull hard. Sometimes he pulled it out. I tried not to cry, because I didn't want him to have that satisfaction, but I usually couldn't help it. When he finally decided he was finished, he would send me to my room.

My room was nothing special, but it was a safe haven. For some reason he never came into my room, although when I heard his footsteps on the stairs, I was sure that this would be the time he would. I curled up in my bed and sobbed. Each time I had survived another beating, I knew that tomorrow would bring more of the same. How could I go on like this? There were no more choices. All the money I had tried to save from babysitting I'd used for clothes for my brothers and I. There were no babysitting jobs in this remote location.

Running away was always on my mind. When I turned 15 I thought about where I could go, how much money I would need, and what would happen to my brothers if I weren't there. The only reason I stayed was because I knew my dad would come looking for me. If he found me he would show no mercy. This might be the beating I would not survive. I had a better chance of helping us by staying.

I had never seen my dad beat Royce or my mom but they were on the receiving end of his verbal attacks. Curt and Duane were somewhat safe; Royce and I always tried to step in to protect them. One day, the three boys and dad were in the barn. After milking a cow, Curt spilled the pail of milk. His anger roused, dad went after him with a pitchfork. Royce stepped between Curt and the pitchfork and informed dad that if he was going to stab anyone it would be him. Royce literally and figuratively threw himself on the sword for his brothers on a regular basis. Now that Royce had started to help dad in the barn, I was sure that dad was beating him too, he would never be able to live up to my dad's expectations. In the house I could watch over him, but in the barn I could not.

One summer, a woman who lived a mile or so up the road started to come down to visit our horses. She began talking to me about the horses and soon she felt like a friend. I felt comfortable enough with her to trust her when she started to ask me about my bruises. She was the very first adult outside of my family that I ever talked to about what was going on inside the four walls of our house. After that, every morning when my dad went to work, she came down to check on us and find out how we had weathered the night before. Sometimes she invited me to her cabin and we just sat by the lake. She accepted me unconditionally. With her I could just be who I was and life was okay. She was there for me and I knew it.

I don't remember her name, but I do remember her long dark flowing hair and olive skin; I thought she looked like a beautiful Indian princess. She moved and talked with the kind of elegance and grace that implied a sense of peace and serenity within. If I could find her, I would tell her what a difference she made in my life and how important her company and acceptance was to me. I've never met anyone like her since; she was a blessing to me at a very bad time. She was my guardian angel.

As we became closer, I described to her what it was like to know I was going to be beaten and how I'd try to prepare for it. I told her how my stomach and chest would tighten and hurt, long before my dad got home. By the time he drove up I could hardly breathe. I'd force my breathing to become shallow to control my emotions. I'd tighten my muscles to make the first blow less painful. In reality you can never prepare for that kind of physical and emotional abuse. It was my conscious minds effort to help myself. I always naively hoped that something I had done well that day would ward off his temper. I had no idea how deep inside him the rage was.

Like everything else good in my life, I constantly worried about my friendship with the Indian princess because I knew the consequences if my dad found out. What he did on a daily basis was bad enough, but if he knew I had told someone, there was no doubt in my mind he would try to kill us. His threats to kill all of us were part of our everyday existence. "I would rather kill you than look at you" was an oft-repeated refrain in our house. And the rage in his eyes left no doubt he had the capacity to do it.

Chapter 6

I first met Tom, — the man who turned my life upside down that quiet Sunday afternoon — when we lived in the house on the lake. I was 14 and he was 20, not an appropriate match age-wise by any stretch of the imagination. I had made only one friend in high school: Tom's sister, Barb. I had confided in Barb about my horrible home life, and she felt she had to tell Tom. Barb often called me just so Tom could talk to me. (Not surprisingly, talking on the phone was never allowed unless my dad was gone.) At age 20, Tom was very mature and compassionate for his age and very consoling in our conversations. On the phone one night Tom asked me out. I was too frightened to ask dad if I could go, so Tom came over and asked my dad himself.

I was very embarrassed about the dilapidated house we lived in and how terribly poor we were, but these things didn't matter to Tom. My dad allowed me to go out with him that night for a couple of hours. I instantly felt comfortable with him. He was a large man who towered over me, but not in an intimidating way. With his arms around me I felt safe and cared for. That night he kissed me softly and gently and for the first time I felt a new kind of love. From then on we were allowed to date occasionally. Each time we went out I told him more and more about my life. He wanted to know everything and I could sense he wanted to protect me.

Although I was not able to contact my grandma when we moved to the farm, again she found us. During our exchange of letters, I told her about Tom. She was not very happy, very concerned about our age difference. She also knew how needy I was and was sure that I would end up pregnant. She pushed me to break up with Tom, certain that there was nothing good about this relationship. As much as I trusted her wisdom, I saw him as my rescuer. I was needy and desperate for his comfort and companionship.

Uncharacteristically, in addition to letting me see Tom, my dad let me join a Girl Scout troop. I could not go to its meetings very often because they met in town, which meant an extra trip into town at night.

One night my dad had some work to do in town so I got to go. He told me that he would pick me up in two hours and I should be waiting by the door. When the meeting ended early, I walked with the others girls to the Rainbow Café. The Rainbow, a popular teen hangout, was full of kids drinking

Cokes and eating French fries. I doubt that I had been invited to go with them, but since all the Girl Scouts went, I was included too. I felt like I belonged, if only by default.

My dad arrived early to pick me up and I was not there. When he finally found me at the Rainbow he was enraged. He walked into the café and headed straight toward me, pushing kids aside as he walked through the crowd. I will never forget the look in his eyes as he plowed through the café. The rage in his eyes burned a hole right through me. His fury was apparent in every part of his body as he made his way toward me. As he came closer, I knew my life was in danger. He grabbed my hair and pulled me out of the booth and pushed me to the floor. As a hush fell over the room, he then yanked me up and shoved me out the door.

He pushed me into the truck and began screaming at me while pounding his fist into my chest as he drove. After we traveled a few miles, he stopped on a deserted country road and yelled at me to get out. The moon was out but it was still pitch black on that road. He might just kill me and leave my body there, I thought. He continued to pummel me until I fell to the road. I lay on the road, and prayed that I would die and that God would take care of my mom and brothers. When I could not get up as fast as he demanded, he pulled me up and shoved me back into the truck. I was hurt badly but there was no one to turn to. I prayed that he was finished, but his rage still boiled and he continued to beat me. Hopelessness is all that I remember feeling. I was exhausted, too broken to even be angry at him.

The lake was another place I found solace. Sometimes after I'd been beaten, I'd wait for my family to fall asleep and sneak out of the house. The walk to the lake was quiet and peaceful. Sometimes, in the clear moonlit sky, I saw a beautiful world. That night, long after my dad fell asleep, I slipped out of the house and headed for the lake. My whole body throbbed as I walked. I needed to sit by the water and weigh my options. My instincts told me that I had a 50/50 chance of surviving if I stayed. If I ran, undoubtedly he would track me down and kill me. The beatings were brutal but every time he took his rage out on me, there was a chance my brothers would be spared. It was worth it. I would stay.

I sat on the sand at the edge of the water and watched the waves roll in and out. Similar to the peace I felt while horseback riding, the motion of the waves calmed me. Even in the moonlight I could see the beauty of the lake. I let the spirit of the lake surround me. In the serenity and peacefulness of the lake I could feel a higher power at work. My grandma had taught me long before that there were blessings even in the most horrible situations. When I was sitting by the water I could believe that there was more to life than what was going on in our family and that maybe, someday, I might find these blessings.

Just across the lake from where I was sitting was Hazelden, a renowned substance abuse treatment center. Maybe I could steal a boat, row over there, knock on the door, and ask them to help us. It was a fanciful thought, but my family desperately needed help. Would this ever end? How much more could we take?

Emotionally I was at a breaking point, crying myself to sleep every single night, even when I wasn't beaten. I wallowed in my worthlessness and wondered why, in the blackness of my world, Tom and the Indian princess were my only glimmer of hope.

We lived in that house for seven or eight months, then one day my dad simply moved us to a different house about four miles away. I suspect we were completely out of money; the electricity and phone had been turned off for awhile, and we had no fuel to cook with or to heat the house.

Our next house had also been abandoned. If possible, it was in worse condition than the previous one. In this house, the only heat came from a single stove in the living room. In the winter, I thought that we might freeze to death which, at the time, seemed like a logical — and somewhat welcome — conclusion that would end the violence.

Unbelievably, my father had managed to isolate us even further. The closest neighbor was at least a quarter mile away. Our house was set back on the property and engulfed by large trees. The cover of the trees made it nearly impossible to see the house from the road. A dirt path served as a driveway and next to the road there was a barn that was on the verge of collapse. Inside the barn, large gaps in the boards revealed the light from the outside. The pattern of the sunshine and shadows gave it a prison-like feel. This was appropriate, since in every way we were my father's prisoners, locked in a world from which there was no escape.

Chapter 7

Just before our last move I had lied about my age and was hired to wash dishes at a popular restaurant in the next town. I was a hard worker and within a week it was clear the owner, Bud, liked me. I soon graduated from dishwasher to waitress, which meant more money.

Bud, and his wife Rose, owned the restaurant. They had no children so their restaurant was the center of their lives. They even lived above it. A few years before, they had come to town to start the cafe. The rumor was that they moved from the Twin Cities but no one really knew anything about them. They never mentioned friends or family. Their past life was a mystery to all of us.

They had worked hard to build a thriving business. I felt lucky to work in such a great place. From the start, I was a popular waitress. Customers requested to sit in my area and I had many regulars who tipped me well.

My dad was pleased that I had gotten such a good paying job. As long as I could do all that was expected of me at home — which was everything — I was allowed to work. However, he wouldn't be inconvenienced by it. Most often I was expected to find my own rides to and from work. Most of the time Tom or another kind soul would chauffeur me. Once again, I was earning enough money to buy a few items of clothing for my brothers and me.

Every Saturday night after work I bought a dollar's worth of their favorite penny candies for each of them. They were asleep when I got home, but the bags of candy would be waiting for them in the morning. I could not always protect them, but I could give them *something* to look forward to. It was a tiny sliver of light behind those prison walls. Even now when my brothers talk about the candy their eyes well up with tears.

I met Judy working at the restaurant. She lived in a nearby town and attended a different school. Although she was a year older than me, we became close friends almost immediately. Judy was friendly and a hard worker who taught me the job. Our personalities just clicked from the start. Small towns have few secrets and though she had never met me she knew about my home life. Soon Judy, her boyfriend Dave, Tom and I were inseparable; we would spend as much time together as I was allowed. We would usually be together after work, hanging out at a park or in a nearby gravel pit. On occasion, we would go to Judy's or Tom's house, but I would never be allowed to bring them to my house; nor would I have wanted to.

The three of them became my pillars of support. They knew what was happening in my home and I knew I finally had friends I could count on. Early in our friendship Judy insisted that Tom and I meet her parents. The night I met them, they declared that I would always be welcome at their house. I could call them anytime, day or night, and they would come to get me. As kind as their offer was, I knew I could never call. It would put them in too much danger. I could never inflict my dad's violence on another family.

My home life continued to worsen, which I didn't think was possible. My dad was in a continuous rage. To terrorize us, he often brought out his shotgun and waved it around as he screamed at us. He'd told us repeatedly that he would much rather shoot us than look at us. One day he decided to make good on his threat.

Returning from work, I walked into the house and found my mom and three brothers lined up against the kitchen sink. Dad stood before them aiming his shotgun at them. I froze, trying to comprehend the scene I'd walked in on. That one split second felt like an eternity. This was the day he'd been talking about — the day that he would kill us. I remember the hatred in his eyes as he screamed at me, but I couldn't hear what he was saying; I was in a daze.

I turned around and ran out the door, certain he would shoot me as I ran. Sprinting to the closest house a quarter mile away, I frequently stumbled and fell. Luckily when I finally got there someone was home. I was crying so hard and was so frantic, I couldn't talk. When I was finally able to blurt what was happening, they called the police.

When my dad realized that I had run for help, he sent Curt after me, ordering him not to come back without me. When Curt couldn't catch me he was afraid to go back to the house for fear of being shot. After a short while, I heard the police sirens as the cars raced to our house. Tom's dad, the county sheriff, was one of the officers that responded. He found my dad sitting out in a field with his gun. What was it like to be so close to the breaking point that you almost killed your whole family? How desperate our situation had become.

How it is that society hadn't intervened to help us, I continually wondered. I was sure that school officials knew about his violence and grasped what was happening to us. They must have known that he was a time bomb just waiting to go off. How did a system that was designed to protect children fail us?

I was too traumatized to respond to the questions that the police asked me. Eventually I was able to talk enough to tell them that I would not go home. I was almost 16 years old, which must have been a magical age in the eyes of the law, because I was able to make that choice and have it accepted. I later learned there was a law in effect that allowed a 16 - year-old to be become an emancipated minor.

A social worker picked me up from the neighbors' house.

When she arrived I could tell she resented having to do this. It was Memorial Day weekend and there was no foster home to put me in, so she took me to her house. She made it evident that I was a burden and was ruining her plans for the long weekend. She gave me a bedroom where, instead of sleeping, I could only stare into the space that extended well beyond the ceiling.

The social worker required me to keep the bedroom door partway open, a clue that she saw I needed some help to process the day's horrific event, yet I was offered none.

It's hard to explain how I felt in the hours and days that followed the event. The tears that had always been a release for me were no longer flowing. I had been pushed beyond my capabilities to process and understand.

In the days that followed, I was told that despite the near-shooting, my dad was allowed to continue to live in the house with my mom and brothers. I couldn't understand why nothing was done to protect my family. What could he have said to convince them that everything would be ok? How could they let my dad stay there after what he had done? It was devastating to know my dad was still there and my family was in danger. It was incomprehensible to me!

This was a turning point in my life. I was completely on my own. If I was going to make my way in this world I was going to have to support myself. I was lucky to have friends I could turn to for emotional support. But I was old beyond my years, and blessed with my Grandmother Selma's wisdom and the power of

God to help me through.

When Tuesday finally came, a family who had heard about what had happened was willing to take me in. I was still dazed, unable to think straight and worried sick about my family. I desperately wanted someone to talk to me, help me and comfort me, yet I felt more like a prisoner than a rescued child. I had no idea how to reach Tom and was unsure if he even knew about the events that had transpired. Because of confidentiality I could not assume his dad had told him.

I desperately wanted the safety of my grandma's arms and for her to hold me like she did when I was a child. But she was two hours away, which felt like 5,000 miles to me then. In my traumatized state I didn't know where I was or how to reach her, and I also knew that I couldn't burden her with this. It would be too much for her.

When I got to the foster family's home I was finally able to see Tom. He held me in his arms and finally all my tears poured out. I thought that they would never stop.

I stayed with the foster family for almost a week but I wasn't happy there. This house was nicer than any home I had ever lived in. The family acted as if like they liked one another. It was so different from what I knew and I felt so out of place there. I didn't know how to function in such a healthy environment. The family was disappointed that I chose not to stay there, but seemed to understand. Sadly for me, I would've felt the same way in another home. The idea of a normal home was foreign to me; I had no idea how to transition to it.

As soon as they heard what had happened, Rose and Bud invited me to live with them. Theirs was a household with its own dysfunction — I knew that they were both alcoholics — but they were nice to me and would still pay me for working in the restaurant. Now that I was on my own, I had to earn money. It felt fairly comfortable there. It would work out. It would have to. I was out of options.

No one explained the court process to me and I didn't understand the details of court, I only knew that I had to appear before a judge to avoid being sent back home. I didn't know that I'd be asked to explain why I shouldn't go home.

The social workers and other adults working on my case talked around me, instead of talking to me. No one addressed my emotional well-being. I was invisible in my own pain. I was treated like someone who had to be "dealt with," someone whose parents had failed in their care, someone who was now a burden to society.

When I walked into the courtroom, my mom and dad were already there. The social worker instructed me to take my place in the chair next to the judge. I sat facing my dad, terrified, sobbing and shaking. As emotional and frightened as I was, I was also still numb from the entire ordeal. In a brave moment I looked up and saw my mom and dad as two broken people with shattered lives. For the first time I could clearly see the wreckage and the hopelessness that was our family. What had become of us? What would happen now? If I were sent home, dad would continue to beat me until he beat the life out of me. If I didn't go home, would he beat the lives out of them instead? I wouldn't survive either way. No wonder I was terrified.

My dad never looked at me as I nervously told the judge how he had verbally and physically abused me and threatened to kill our family. Then, drawing on all the courage I could muster, I told the judge that I could not return home. I wasn't the only one who knew my dad would kill me if I went home; I sensed the judge knew it too. He talked to me in such a way that made me think he was aware of dad's great anger toward my grandmother, knowing that my living with her would result in more violence at home.

I was lucky; he decided I did not have to go back. I was placed in the custody of Bud and Rose. When the hearing was over, my dad slammed his fist on the table and walked out of the courtroom. My mom came over and told me if I came home, everything would be fine. "Why did you choose to make trouble for our family?" she asked. She was right: I did make trouble. But finally our family secret of abuse was out in the open. Would we finally get some help?

The guilt I felt over leaving my brothers with no one to protect them overwhelmed me. I worried day and night about them. It was not hard for me to imagine how terrible things might be for them.

Living with Rose and Bud above the restaurant felt more

comfortable than my foster home, but there was nothing about it that resembled a home. Bud and Rose spent all their waking hours in the restaurant, so the upstairs was simply a place to shower and sleep. Rosie, as we called her, was very sweet, but overworked. She would get up every day at 5:00 a.m. to start baking the daily supply of pies for which the restaurant was famous. Everything they served was homemade.

Rosie did the work and Bud "supervised." He often told us the story of how he'd been shot in the knee and couldn't be on his feet for long. To the employees, it sounded like an excuse not to work. Most days he smoked cigarettes, gossiped with the customers and drank.

It was hard to feel like I fit in with a family story like mine following me around. After all, this was a small town and the story had spread quickly. It was hard to go to school where everyone knew what had happened. My brothers were in a different part of the same school but I didn't know how to arrange to see them. What would I say to them when all I wanted to do was rescue them? I could only worry about them.

I had been living with Rose and Bud only a short time when I realized that my new home might end up being as bad as the home I left. One day when I was alone in the kitchen, Bud came up behind me and put his arms around me. He touched my breasts and kissed my neck. I could feel his hard penis pressed into my back. I pulled away, but the more I tried to pull away the more he confined me. Then someone came into the kitchen and he let go, acting as if nothing had happened.

Had I done something to make him do this to me? I had beautiful long blond hair and a nice shape. My breasts were large and my small waist accentuated them more. Because of this I thought I had enticed him in some way. From then on I studiously avoided being alone anywhere in the restaurant. Unfortunately he would sometimes find me and force me into the back room. He'd then push me into a corner, unzip his pants and make me touch him and arouse him. I wanted to throw up. I didn't know how to get away. I desperately needed the money this job provided. This is what I deserved, I thought. This hell was the price I had to pay to get out of my father's hell.

Bud was a tall and very thin man of about 50, though he looked much older. He had dark hair and a prominent widow's peak. His small eyes and the lines in his face made him look angry all the time. This is how I pictured the devil might look. Even before his abuse began I always felt uneasy around him. Though I never expected him to hurt me, I never quite trusted him either.

One night I woke to find him in my room. He grabbed my trembling hands and held them firmly above my head, demanding that I be quiet. I sobbed uncontrollably as he raped me. Afterwards, paralyzed with fear, shock and pain, I couldn't comprehend what had happened. But I knew, once again, I had a secret to keep.

Is this what I owed him for food and shelter? If not, I must have done something horrible to deserve this. Since

I already knew that I was a terrible person, that nothing good would ever come to me, and that I was completely worthless, this made sense. How stupid was I to think that this place was going to be good? Did I really think that I wouldn't have to pay a price for food, clothing and a decent roof over my head?

At least from here I could see an escape route. I would find some way out — some path to a better life. At 16, I felt like I had lived many lifetimes already. If I could hang on until I got my high school diploma, I could go to college like I had dreamed of and then I would be in a better position help my family and create a better life for myself. On good days I could see the light amidst the darkness and imagine that my dream might come true.

One of Royce's responsibilities was to drive the tractor towing a wagon of feed to the small town where I worked. The trip to town was at least 10 miles, which took a long time with a tractor and trailer. Of course it was my father's expectation that Royce could handle such adult responsibilities even though he was only 11 years old.

While the feed was being ground, Royce came to the cafe. He was extremely thin and wore a threadbare coat that was not nearly warm enough. His jeans were too short to cover his skinny legs and his shoes were so tattered I couldn't tell what was holding them together. Whenever he came into the restaurant, Bud would tell him that he couldn't talk to me and ordered him to get out because he didn't have money to buy anything. For this I stood up to Bud, so he would let my brother stay. I knew

I would suffer for it later.

I would always buy Royce a cheeseburger, French fries, and malt. Before he left I made up three bags of candy for him to take home for himself and my brothers. It wasn't much, but it was all I could do. Royce had to hide the candy when he brought it into the house. Not surprisingly, if dad found out that Royce stopped to see me it would be the start of another rampage.

When he left I would cry so hard I was sure my heart would break in two. He did not have to tell me, I could see in his eyes what he was going home to. Neither grandma nor the legal system was able to get my brothers out of there. Doing so would most certainly cost them their lives. If I told grandma that I was being raped, it would surely kill her. My world was so dark. I had been in this place before. It was a place of such desolation and despair, my spirit was completely extinguished. The pain and loss were nearly too much to bear. As it had many times before, suicide loomed as an option.

The room where I slept had only a curtain as a door so I never had any privacy. My desperate wish for a door with a lock on it was only a dream. Bud was coming into my room at least once a week to rape me, sometimes more often. He always came in the middle of the night. After a while, I could hear him get out of bed before his feet even hit the floor. I cried and prayed that he was just going to the bathroom and wouldn't come into my room, but he always did. Rosie, in her alcohol-assisted coma, never heard.

Chapter 8

A social worker visited me from time to time, when I lived with Rose and Bud. This was the same social worker I went home with the day my dad tried to kill us. My previous experience led me to believe that I was a pain in the ass to her as well as society, and her attitude hadn't changed. I was still a second-class citizen.

Each time she came to visit me I thought "this will be the time to tell her that Bud is raping me." Bud was also aware that I might do this, and always made sure that he was within earshot; he always instructed me where to sit when I talked to her, so it was impossible to tell her without Bud knowing about it. Not that I had much of a chance to tell her. Her visits were brusque, at best. She never looked at me when she talked to me. Since it was clear I had as much value as dirt, I was afraid that if I did tell her she'd tell me I deserved it. "How could we expect anything different from someone coming from a family like yours?" she'd say. And I'd know she was right.

Judy suspected something was wrong and one day she confronted me. "You'd better tell me what's going on because I won't stop asking you until I know." The time had come; I could not hide it anymore — it had been going on almost a year and a half. Though the money I was earning was my ticket out of there, I couldn't take being raped anymore. During Bud's assaults I shut down emotionally and numbly tolerated what came my way. Every month I anxiously waited for my period, and worried what would happen to me if I got pregnant?

Judy started to cry when I told her about Bud. It was hard for her to hear, although a part of her knew it was happening. She noticed that Bud was often very critical of my work, to the point that she confronted him about how I was being treated. The other waitresses were treated much more fairly than I was. I was given more special orders and tables than I could handle. He would often let the other waitresses leave early so I would have to do all the clean-up myself. It was her instinct that I was being punished that led her to confront me in the first place. Immediately she orchestrated what needed to happen next. She called Tom, who came right over. Together we told him what had been happening. I'll never forget the look of horror on his face and the wrath in his eyes.

Once again my life laid in pieces before me. I was broken and helpless; I would never feel whole again. My friends knew I needed adults to help me. Judy took me to her house where we told her parents. I remember so clearly how I sat at their kitchen table as Judy, Dave, Tom, and Judy's parents made a protective circle around me. I sobbed and told them about Bud's ongoing sexual assaults. My whole body shook but I could feel their love surround me. Orin, Judy's dad, gently held my hand and said "Sandy, we have to call the sheriff. Do you understand?" I did. "You'll stay with us. We love you and will protect you like our own." Then he hugged me and told Tom to call and ask his dad to come over.

Over the next few days I was swarmed by police and court-appointed lawyers who asked me countless questions that I did my best to answer. Then after the initial inquiries, it felt like the case was just dropped.

It wasn't until 30 years later that I learned that lawyers had been appointed to prosecute my case but in the end it was Bud's word against mine. He was a prominent business owner and I was a girl from a poverty stricken, abusive, dysfunctional home, now in custody of the state. Bud had been scared and hired a team of lawyers to defend him, but in the end he was never brought to justice.

Despite all the trauma I'd endured, I was never offered counseling. I didn't even know how or what to ask for. I *did* know that I was deeply and severely wounded. This was just another one of the many deep wounds, which would be added to the others, that may never heal.

Judy's parents kept their promise: They treated me like their daughter, they gave me a place to stay, but were unable to help me financially. I was grateful for food and shelter and would never ask them for money. Judy was in college when I moved in. I was about to turn 18 and graduate from high school so I had to figure out how to support myself. Would I be able to do that and go to college?

As a high school senior I was confused over what direction to go. Judy encouraged me to go to college like she was doing. As much as I had dreamed of this, it seemed as unlikely as winning the lottery. Judy, however, did not give up easily and urged me not to give up the dream and to make college my goal. My guidance counselor, Mr. Myers, was more skeptical. He knew my background; he had counseled me many times about my bruises and had often encouraged me to get out of our house. He pointed out all that was working against me: My grades were below average; I was emotionally unstable; I had no financial or family support. On paper I wasn't the ideal college candidate, but he started the process anyway.

He'd underestimated my commitment to finding a better life. I had decided that nothing and no one would get in the way of achieving it. It's a good thing I didn't do what Mr. Myers had done and looked at this goal from a logical perspective, because I would have gone down in defeat immediately.

Somehow I had acquired more determination than I knew I had. When I was accepted to Mankato State College, I was both elated and petrified. Mr. Myers gave me one last "realistic" talk about how difficult he thought college would be for me. My newfound determination was intoxicating. "If you think I can't do it," I challenged, "just watch me!"

Two days after my high school graduation, I received a letter from him telling me I was awarded a scholarship that would pay for half a year of college. Apparently he believed in me after all. It seemed as though my life was finally moving forward. I was looking forward to joining Judy in Mankato in the fall and I was optimistic about everything.

Judy and Dave got engaged my senior year and planned to marry the next July. Although I never had a ring, Tom and I had also made a commitment to each other. Years earlier he had promised to love and take care of me forever. I believed him and completely trusted him with my heart, the heart that I was so protective of. I had never loved anyone the way I loved him. I was sure of our future together.

On the night of Judy and Dave's wedding, Tom abruptly broke off our engagement and left me. He offered no explanation. I never spoke to him again until he called me that Sunday afternoon in April, 30 years later.

I had no place to go for this summer so I called and asked grandpa and grandma if I could stay with them. Despite my recent victories, I had been through much trauma since they'd last seen me several years before. The girl that they picked up was severely damaged, more broken than they ever imagined.

Though I was thrilled to be in a safe place where I knew I

was loved, I had constructed walls around myself that were too thick to penetrate. Even grandma couldn't enter the fortress that I had created. I couldn't accept her love. This was the first time in my life I couldn't share my pain with Grandma Selma, and it hurt me immensely not be honest with her. It was then that I decided that I would never again allow anyone into my heart. I would protect it with every bit of energy I had so no one could ever hurt me again.

That fall I started my freshman year with a new attitude. I would prove that I was just as good as everyone else. If I never again acknowledged my past, steered clear of conversations about childhood or family, I would be an equal. It was important to me to do whatever it took to be like everyone else. I became highly skilled at letting people get only so close and then letting them get no further.

In the fall, I began my freshman year and moved into a college dorm. Within the first month I was there my dad called me. I don't how he found me. I hadn't spoken to him since I left more than two years ago, and nothing had changed with him. He was enraged and threatened to come to my room that day and kill me. That familiar terror again gripped me as I went to Judy's room for help. We were both aware that he was capable of carrying out his threat; Judy knew we had to tell the dorm supervisor. Together they convinced me that I had no choice but to call the police — he had proven he was just too dangerous to ignore. The police came to the dorm to ask me questions, and then decided I needed to come to the station with them. It was embarrassing to walk through the lobby escorted by the police. My dad never came to school but I lived every minute fearing he would. As hard as I tried to block them out, the memories and the pain were always present, haunting me.

This same year my dad moved the family to a farm 10 miles outside of Pine City. The house was in better condition than any other place my family had lived, but there was still no central heat or running water. Though I never lived there, I know life continued to be a challenge for my brothers.

Not long after this move, my dad left permanently — with another woman. Before leaving, he told Royce that he was taking him and his brothers with him. If he had Royce's cooperation, he knew that my other brothers would go willingly too. He warned Royce that they'd be leaving within a day or two and to have their bags packed. Royce played along until the time came to go, and then he firmly stated, "We're not going." He knew that this would be the very last time he'd ever be beaten.

Except for Royce's visits to the cafe, I had not seen anyone else in the family since the day I left. The first time I went to Pine City to see them I also had to appear in court as part of my parents' divorce proceedings. With my dad gone, it made it possible for us to reunite as a family. They were living in poverty but at least they were safe. Mom still suffered from debilitating depression and lived on public assistance. My brothers got odd jobs to help out. I would send money as often as I could from my college loan money. We were finally moving forward to a better life.

Chapter 9

During the first week of my freshman year I met Jerry, the man I would eventually marry. I sat next to him, or more accurately, tripped over him trying to get to my seat in a crowded classroom. He was quite handsome, a sharp dresser and I was impressed. Though he showed great interest in me, I gave no indication that the interest was reciprocal and remained merely polite. But he persisted in his loving, kind, gentle, and patient way, and eventually he won me over. Though I loved Jerry, I remained faithful to my pledge to never be hurt again, and sealed off a good part of my heart.

That school year also brought more things I didn't anticipate. Going to college had been my dream yet Mr. Myer's concerns turned out not to be unfounded. I found I was not academically prepared for the rigors of higher education. I was literally failing every class and was soon put on academic probation. My grades were so poor I was not allowed to register for the next quarter.

When I finally confided in my friend and roommate Carna, she said, "You have to march right into the dean's office and do whatever it takes to get back in school." She went with me to make sure I did. I poured my heart out to the dean, confessing the story of my life, counting on his kindness. It worked. He agreed to reinstate me for one quarter.

Carna, a straight A student, forced me to accompany her to the library every night to raise my grade point average. I studied with her all year and by spring quarter my grade point was a respectable C+ average. Her directive had worked. My improved grades got me to be admitted to the Social Work Department where I was also given a job. The professor I worked for was the head of American Indian studies. Though I was an undergraduate, he treated me like a graduate student. This was a big responsibility and it gave me a huge boost of much needed confidence.

I continued to deal with my past the only way I knew how — I ignored it. I had become extremely adept at suppressing my emotions. Despite a few setbacks, my dream was happening and I was changing the course of my life.

The lives of my brothers were also moving forward, at least more forward than ever before. Now the boys were old enough to have jobs and financially things looked a little better. I spent summers at my grandparents and Royce often brought the rest of the family to see us.

With my dad gone, my grandparents were free to try to fix

the broken pieces. Unfortunately they lived hours away and were getting on in years, but they helped financially by paying off the farm, they tried to get help for my mom, and they supported us the best they could.

My brothers were survivors and knew how to work and earn a buck. Like me, they were years older than their chronological ages. Also like me, they'd had their own guardian angels that had helped and guided them through their childhoods, and they remain close to these people today. Royce, Curt and Duane have their own collection of stories to tell about the many people who helped them. It is my hope that one day they will tell their stories.

Chapter 10

Incredibly, I made it over all the hurdles, and despite the odds, my dream was realized. I graduated from college and accepted a job in social work. Eventually I moved to the Twin Cities to live with my college roommate and be near my boyfriend Jerry. I had lived with Carna for only a few days when out of the blue, I got a call from my dad. I had not talked to him since the day of his threatening call my freshman year. Unwittingly I had moved only three blocks away from him.

This time he was calm and conversational. There was no sign of the angry violent father I'd always known. He had remarried and wanted us to forget the past and be one big happy family. Though he acted "normal", I would never trust him. Just hearing his voice made me feel vulnerable and fearful. I found ways to avoid his calls and thanked God that he never came to the house, although I was always worried that he might. I worked all day and then spent evenings and weekends with

Jerry, which offered me a sense of security.

Jerry and I had been dating for three years. I knew that he might eventually ask me to marry him. This presented me with a problem because I had decided to never get married. I'm not sure when I made that decision, but I knew that I never wanted children, or that I would ever rely on any one for financial or emotional support again. That is why I never told Jerry my story. I wanted to be completely self-sufficient, and would never, ever depend on anyone for anything. I loved children but I was scared to make the same mistakes that my parents had.

Jerry and I were married in October of 1974. I can't tell you for sure what made me change my mind; even then I must have realized that my strong stance was unrealistic and unhealthy. Jerry was, and still is, a loving, kind and supportive man who loved me despite a past I never talked about.

When my long-suppressed past emerged, this man had the patience to allow me to become who I would become. Jerry weathered the storm and accepted all my baggage that washed up on shore. I'd never told him about my life and how bad it was and he never pressured me for the details, which is how I wanted it. My brothers were just as skilled at keeping our secrets as I was. We all thought that this was the right way to handle our painful past.

Having kids was something I did not want to do, because I had no idea how to raise them. Without any role models, I knew nothing about how to be a good parent. But Jerry and I have three almost-grown sons who are smart, popular and active in school and community. I can't imagine life without them.

When the boys were young we lived in a close-knit neighborhood where most of the moms stayed home. I worked part-time so I could be home too. Almost every day we neighborhood moms would take our kids to the park or get together for play groups. These were great moms and I watched them carefully, emulating everything they did. Early childhood education classes had just been introduced and I attended every session I could. In class I would learn everything from infant care to the best way to discipline kids. I read every child-raising book I could find. I modeled every good behavior and soon I was feeling somewhat confident. Friends commented on what a good mother I was. I had leaped over another hurdle.

By now my brothers were grown and mom had left the farm and moved closer to her parents and other relatives. It was comforting to all of them to be closer to each other again.

Each time I saw him grandpa kept telling me that he wouldn't be around for my wedding. My wedding was almost 10 months away and I certainly did not want to think about his death, although unconsciously I thought it might be true. He would sit in his favorite chair and remark that the wedding would have to go on without him. His intuition proved right and he passed away three months before my wedding.

Grandma Selma died about four years after grandpa. I was devastated, but consistent with the way I've always buried my sadness, I didn't really mourn her death. I felt numb and empty, but it also provided me with yet another excuse to keep running forward and not look back. The influence her spiritual guidance had on me didn't entirely reveal itself until I began to examine my past.

After my grandparents died, mom moved back to Pine City where she had many friends. My mom's life had always been filled with many devoted friends. I was always amazed at the large number of friends she had given how little she got out. When she was unable to leave the house, she communicated with friends by phone, sometimes starting her calls at 6 AM. Keeping in contact with her friends was a way to gauge how depressed she was. If they hadn't heard from her in a while they would call us and check in. She'd given more attention and showed more love to them than she ever showed my brothers and me — at least that's what we saw from our childs' viewpoint.

She ended up living a simple but comfortable life of her choosing. She did exactly as she wanted to do and I always strongly encouraged her to make her own decisions. Many times however that caused a great deal of pain for me because her choices were made from a place of deep depression. I found it painful to watch her emotionally and physically sink deeper and deeper into herself. Many times she would not take her medication, go to the doctor, or eat healthy. Soon she had diabetes and congestive heart failure, along with her high blood pressure. As time passed, her physical condition worsened but her depression improved slightly, although she still suffered several debilitating bouts each year. The worst of these always started in late fall and stayed until late spring. All in all, she was happier than she'd ever been.

All three of my brothers found wonderful wives to whom they are still married. They too managed to rise above their childhood and raise their children exactly the opposite of the way we were brought up. Though each of us has had our share of problems, amazingly we all lead normal lives, have raised healthy children and created happy, high-functioning families.

Of course while I was living my adult existence, I was also hiding from the many emotional upheavals of my childhood. I lived in constant fear of not being good enough so I worked diligently to make sure my performance went beyond what was expected of me in every aspect of my life. I became an active school and community volunteer who oversaw large, significant projects. People viewed me as a skilled leader, enthusiastic speaker, and an all-round positive person with a great laugh. No one would have ever imagined my turbulent childhood.

Over the years, I lost contact with Judy and Dave. The call from Tom gave me a reason to reconnect with them. It turned out that Tom had found me through them. Judy confided that this was not the first time Tom had tried to find me. He had called her just a month before my wedding and again several years later. Each time Judy stood firm and wouldn't tell him my whereabouts. She refused to give him my address but this time she gave him my married name, which was the clue he needed to find me. He called me within 20 minutes of talking to her.

I had convinced myself that my past was buried too deeply to ever find its way out. Still another part of me knew that someday I would have to face — and make peace with— my past. That time was at hand.

The Journey to Forgiveness and Peace

The completed journey always ends with a return, a homecoming to the ordinary world of conventional reality that was left behind. This world has been transformed, if our journey has been successful, into a new world, seen with fresh eyes. The end of the journey is the beginning of a new, empowered way of life.

- Ralph Metzner

Chapter 11

Is it really possible to heal from all the trauma I've endured? I had no idea; I had struggled with that question most of my life. Muriel told me it was possible, but I'm not sure I believed it. But I wanted my wounds to heal more than anything else. How it would happen was uncertain. I would soon learn that healing is a journey that unfolds on its own schedule.

"Each and every one of us has all the resources inside of us to heal our body, mind and spirit," said Muriel. I sensed this was true even if I didn't yet know how it could be.

I knew nothing about what lay on the healing road ahead, except that it would be painful. The pain was the very reason I'd kept my secret, and never attempted to make peace with this before. Now, for the first time, the pain of hiding my past was greater than the pain of exposing it.

Coming to grips with my past was not just emotionally exhausting, but took a huge physical toll as well. Since the day that Tom had called I had hardly slept and I started having constant near-migraine headaches. None of the usual medications worked so I visited a chiropractor who used "Trigger Point" therapy. This released the tension in my neck that was causing the headaches, and I was able to keep them under control without medication.

My blood pressure skyrocketed and as a result I needed medication. All my issues were trapped in the cells of my body. The physical manifestations provided another good reason to finally face my past. I was ready to begin.

As my story spilled out, it felt like every moment in Muriel's office was spent crying. I was so emotional that I felt nauseated days before appointments. I usually had to force myself to go, worried that I might throw up enroute. I was on an emotional roller coaster that was out of control. I would fall asleep crying every night and wake up crying every morning.

The intensity of my emotion frightened me. Would I retreat to my bedroom with a nervous breakdown like my mother had? Was I going crazy? I viewed my oceans of tears as a sign of weakness when in fact they were a sign of healing. The amount of emotion that had been pent up in my body and was now being released was frightening.

This release of tears without restriction allowed my body to clear itself of the toxins that were stored inside. I know now that it was good for me, but at the time I was afraid I would not ever be able to pull myself out of this mire of depression.

If it is true that the eyes are the windows to the soul, surely mine revealed the intolerable sadness inside me. Now others would see the vulnerabilities that I'd been hiding. But it was too late now; they were no longer hidden. My massive quantities of tears symbolized the truth. In human experience, your emotions ebb and flow like the waves. Allowing me to feel my own pain was an unconscious choice my body made when it could no longer contain it.

I began having flashbacks so real it was if I was living through the trauma all over again. I would wake in the middle of the night terrified, thinking I was still a child being beaten by my dad. The flashbacks transported me back in time and I was unaware of my current surroundings. I would find myself curled up in a ball, like I did when I was a child, protecting myself as I felt his every blow. Jerry could only watch helplessly; there was nothing he could do to console me. As hard as it was, this was a process I had to go through myself. When they finally subsided, I came back to reality but I suffered after-effects much longer. After a flashback I was drained of energy and I found it impossible to focus. I walked around in a daze. Even worse, the emotions that accompanied my flashbacks stayed with me for days, like a black cloud surrounding me. These were among the scariest experiences I have ever been through.

The flashbacks began shortly after I started therapy. I had assumed that therapy would start "working" immediately, and didn't understand why I was feeling worse. Now I was faced with an unbearable reality: I could not go back in hiding. My only choice was to move forward.

Muriel's depth of understanding was evident in her compassion and care. This is what kept me going every other week. Unearthing my story was a sacred task, a task that needed to be done with compassion, and I knew she had that compassion. Although I knew I was in capable hands, I didn't yet completely trust her. This wasn't surprising — I had little reason to trust anyone, especially with matters of my heart. After each session I would look for some excuse not to go back, usually based on something she might say.

As much as I was looking for a way out, I was also looking for a way in and I had found it in Muriel. She was always completely present and nonjudgmental and I could feel that. I would have to learn to trust her enough to let her guide me to the depths of my soul and then back out again.

As I tentatively unearthed each piece of my story from the darkness of my soul, I could feel my energy change. A burden was being lifted as I finally shared my long-kept secrets. Little by little I could feel the shift. My life no longer felt as dark and shameful as it once did.

At this same time Royce was struggling with similar issues. Shortly after I started working with Muriel, Royce's wife Sue came to see me and asked me questions about our childhood. We talked until late into the night, and I told her everything. Royce had also kept his childhood secret. Sue, like all of our spouses, knew our childhood had been a struggle but had no idea the extreme abuse we'd lived with. Our conversation brought to light a lot of my brother's issues and helped her to understand what was going on inside him. Sue was relieved that I was getting help and expressed hope that my healing journey might bring healing to my brothers as well.

Sue and I could now talk openly on the childhood topic, but I wasn't ready to talk to Royce, and he certainly wasn't ready to talk to me. We both needed more time to figure out our own feelings. It wasn't until almost a year later that Royce suggested that we talk. All four of us are very intuitive, leading me to believe that not only Royce but Curt and Duane were also dealing with our childhood on some level. Hopefully my conversation with Royce would open the door for all of us to talk about this in the future.

I was extremely nervous talking to my brother. He shared my father's bad temper and I couldn't anticipate his reaction to our conversation. His perception of what happened might be totally different than mine. He might be angry with me for leaving them. In the midst of my own healing, I was still feeling very vulnerable. This felt like opening another Pandora's Box.

When the day came I almost backed out. This conversation was long overdue, but now I didn't think I had the courage to go through with it. But I was learning how to do the hard things in life and had to trust that the reward would be greater than the risk. Despite how excruciating it was to finally talk about our horrible childhoods, we did. We talked for most of the day, while Sue sat quietly and listened. At times we all cried together as different parts of our stories came to light. I shared things that he was too young to remember and he recalled events that I had blocked out. Together, we acknowledged our long — buried past and our painful feelings about it. It was interesting to me how we had both coped with our experiences similarly. He had also believed it was best to suppress the memories and move forward, but now it was getting harder and harder for him to hide his emotions and it was time for him to find his own peace.

Chapter 12

In our search for answers, separately both Royce and I had gone back to the locations where the abuse had occurred. I didn't know what I expected to happen, but I could hear a whispering voice telling me to go.

I parked on the road near the lake in Lindstrom that had provided such comfort to me. Maybe if I sat there I would be hit by some insight or understanding. Perhaps my questions would magically be answered and I would find the peace I was looking so hard for. How wonderful it would be to have an epiphany that would give understanding to all that had happened. At best — this was wishful thinking.

The tremendous guilt I felt for leaving my brothers when I left home continued to haunt me. I didn't understand why I hadn't fought for them after my escape. Every time I thought about this I hated myself even more for my selfishness. If all of us couldn't have gotten out, I shouldn't have left either. What I had done was so awful that I could not feel any compassion for myself. What I had done was unforgivable.

Muriel carefully guided me through questions that allowed me to see what was possible then and what was not. I had just turned 16. It wasn't fair to judge what I did then against what I know now as an adult. I must learn compassion for the girl who was 16 and barely able to take care of herself. I had to realize that the 16-year old me did the best she could at the time.

Through guided imagery I went back in time to the age of 16. I visualized myself then as though this was a girl I didn't know. I imagined what it looked like and felt like to be a teenager in such a traumatic situation. As an adult I could relate this to my own son who was the same age. I would not expect him to be capable of all the responsibility of rescuing an entire family from turmoil. It took many, many months to work through this guilt because of how deeply imbedded this was. It made sense that I did not have the resources to take care of my brothers, but my heart still held the guilt.

In visualization I pictured a healing ray of light coming into my body, permeating its every cell and especially my heart. I would sit in a comfortable chair with my feet on the floor. Sometimes soft music would be playing in the background and I would light a candle. Closing my eyes, focusing on my breathing, I would take deep breaths that went down to my belly, and then I would slowly exhale. Doing this until my breathing was rhythmic and my heart rate slowed, I would feel relaxed.

As the ray of light entered my body, I imagined all of my negative energy leaving my body, allowing my unconscious mind to quiet and letting any wisdom come into my awareness that I needed to know, I visualized letting go of anything that no longer served me. Finally, I imagined how this energy from God and the universe would benefit and ground me, always taking all the time I needed — this isn't an endeavor one can rush through — to slowly open my eyes. Then I would take a few minutes to reorient myself and notice all the ways I felt different.

This is a wonderful, healing visualization I still use. It allows me to let my guard down, open my heart, and feel love and compassion for myself. This love and compassion is what enabled me to judge for myself what had happened and stop blaming myself for it. It allowed me to forgive those who hurt me. Ultimately, it meant loving the people who hurt me as well. As grandma had taught me, they were created with the same loving hand that created me. Now I was finally beginning to understand it.

The forgiveness issue was a huge one. Muriel and I worked on it for a long time but I still was not completely finished with it. One question I struggled most with was "why I had not persisted with the social worker until something was done to help my family?"

Royce and I had been unable to talk about this in our recent conversation, so I was still worried about it. Royce was willing to meet with Muriel and me. This meant I would have to face him and tell him how guilty I felt for leaving him and my brothers. He didn't know what my life had been like and I didn't know what theirs had been like. This was a very painful and difficult kind of conversation to have, but it was very much needed.

The conversation started with me. I poured out my guilt over leaving them, telling Royce how I hated myself for not trying to get them out. How I had I worried night and day about them. I was finally able to let him know that once I left home, my life had not been what I had expected. I told him about how Bud had repeatedly raped me. Yet still I felt that this was not a good excuse for not fighting for them. Tears streamed down my face as I asked him if he could ever forgive me.

Royce admitted that he always thought I had been the lucky one for getting out. My heart broke as he explained what the days were like after I left. He'd always thought I would come back to get them, he said. When days turned into weeks and then months, he came to the realization that I wasn't coming back for them and he didn't understand why. As he spoke I could feel the pain and sadness all over again, as if it was happening in the present time.

After I left home, my name was never spoken again. Nonetheless it was undeniable how angry my dad was at me for exposing what was happening in our family. Royce told me that he had so hoped I would come back to get them but intuitively he knew the minute I walked out that I could never go back. By leaving, I had burned that bridge. It was as clear to Royce as it was to me that dad would have killed me if I'd come back. And he would have killed my brothers rather than let them go.

Divine intervention had played a vital role in protecting us. God had provided my brothers and me with the wherewithal to protect ourselves. He also bestowed us with the wisdom to know that we had to create better lives for ourselves. God had directed our paths. The strong feeling I had inside of me told me it was too dangerous to fight for my brothers. Now I can see that it was the hand of God. He guided and kept us safe during this horrible time. How interesting that the hand that I thought was punishing us was really protecting us.

The months since I had started therapy had been tough. Many times I was overwhelmed by depression. I felt lost, alone and confused. My former self no longer existed and didn't know who I would become or how everything would fit together. I felt distant from everyone and everything.

Chapter 13

From the time Tom had called, my life had been in turmoil. Now, almost nine months later, nothing was the same; everything I thought and felt had changed.

Friendships have always been very important to me and I cherish these relationships. I have always been lucky to have many friends who love and support me. They were there to support me through my current trials if I would allow it, but I was not yet at a place yet where I could share what was troubling me. I was also uncertain how to accept any love and compassion that might come my way.

I had confided my situation to a few close friends, including Betsy, Jane and Elaine. It was still too hard to talk about any of this with Jerry and it would be hard for him as well. Neither of us knew how to communicate about something so difficult.

There was still much healing to take place but I no longer felt as powerless as I once had. It was time to take the next step, which was to see Tom. I knew that I had to talk to him in person. There was too much to say and too much to resolve to have a phone conversation.

My friends were very concerned with my plan to see Tom and did not hesitate to tell me so. In fact, they were adamantly against it, and Muriel strongly agreed with them. I valued their opinion; they were all wise women who only wanted what was best for me. They were concerned because they saw the terrible time I'd been having and were concerned that I wasn't making a rational decision. They were also unsure of what motivated Tom to call me. Actually it wasn't clear to me either. This was one of the issues he and I needed to discuss.

My friends and Muriel had my best interests at heart — I shared their concerns — but I knew Tom and I had to talk face-to-face. Though 30 years had gone by, when he called it was as though no time had passed. We had talked as the soul mates we were. What would happen when we were together? I was afraid that if he kissed me or tried to console me that I might melt into his arms. Good intentions might give way to the same feelings that fueled our relationship all those years ago.

I'd always found Tom easy to talk to. Our previous relationship had been built on his taking care of me. Now he thought I was once again in need of his help and support in this healing process. His intentions were not clear, but then I wasn't in a place where I could have a healthy perspective about it. According to Tom, his purpose was to help me heal but my friends disagreed. Was I playing with fire or was fire playing with me? Truthfully, it was some of both.

Before I made any further decisions, I talked to Jerry about my need to see Tom. My marriage and family is not something I would put in jeopardy so it was important to me that he support this meeting. He wasn't surprised. He expected that this was something that I would have to do at some point. Trusting and gracious, Jerry understood what I needed to do. I'm not sure I would have been able to be so generous had the situation been reversed.

The person that Tom had last known was a vulnerable and broken 19-year-old. Then he was my protector and my sole comforter. Did he want to play that role again? My friends were sure he did, but I wasn't. Now it was important that he saw me as a person who could take care of her own problems. I didn't want to see him and fall apart in his arms, hoping he would again come to my rescue. Muriel pointed out that this is exactly how affairs begin. I was fully aware that things can go in a different direction despite the best intentions when someone is emotionally needy.

Muriel suggested that I make some rules to govern our meeting. My first concern was that if he hugged me I might fall apart in his embrace, confirming my need for his help or bringing back romantic feelings. It was important that I not let him touch me. I also had to remember that I was in control. I could end the conversation and leave whenever I felt I needed to.

We were meeting at a coffee house and I pledged to myself that I would not go anywhere else with him. Tom liked to eat out and I thought he might suggest we go out to dinner. The idea of a change in places, Muriel and I thought again, would make me feel too vulnerable.

We talked about how I might feel to see Tom after all this time. While I hoped to convey an image of confidence and independence, I was uncertain how I would respond to him when we actually met. I was feeling very anxious and nervous over this meeting.

When the day finally came I displayed a confidence I didn't know I possessed. It encompassed my entire being. Even my co-workers, who knew nothing about what was going on in my life, noticed the change in me that day. "You look awesome," they told me. They complimented my clothes, my hair and even my make-up. They teased me that I must have something very important to do.

Finally, after more than 30 years, the time had come to see the man who had once been my rescuer and fiancé. It was time to get answers to the questions that were never asked and to ask the questions that would hopefully lead to understanding and provide some closure to our past.

I arrived at the coffee house first and settled at a table. As I waited for Tom I closed my eyes, reminded myself of my intentions for our meeting, and said a silent prayer. I prayed for guidance and compassion as we resolved our past and determined what this meant for our future. God was present; I could feel His peace and knew I wasn't alone. I had set my intention and the energy of the universe was aligned with that purpose. I was ready.

I watched him walk by the window. He looked just like I remembered. As he walked toward me I still felt more confident and secure than I had in a long time. He approached the table and I got up to hug him, breaking my first rule. It was good to see him. I didn't fall apart in his arms like I thought I might.

We talked for almost three hours. Our conversation did not go as I expected. I had anticipated meeting someone who was strong and secure in his present situation. Instead, for most of the night he cried and I consoled him. If I'd been clear-headed myself, I would have seen how insecure he was just from his phone call. Part of his struggle, I believe, was with his role as a healer. God had called him to help people heal, especially me. This role was forcing him to live in the past rather than the present.

It became evident as we talked that Tom desired a relationship that I could not give him. This made it clear that it was impossible for me to pursue a friendship with him. I could see how easy it would be to cross the line.

It was painful for me to hear that he had such deep regret over leaving me. There was a time I wanted to marry him more than anything else but I now knew that God put Tom in my life to protect me then and help me heal now. Although I had once wanted a future with him, this was no longer the case. Though our love had been strong enough to last a lifetime, this was a different place and a different time. We had made other choices, we had separate lives, and we were different people. While Tom believed his purpose in my life still included a relationship between us, it was my belief that we were in each other's lives for other reasons, and it was not to be together. It was to help each other heal from the tragedies and regrets of our pasts.

Tom explained more to me about why he disappeared from my life. His parents had wanted someone better for their son — someone without all my problems. With a family life like mine, they were convinced that I would never amount to anything.

Tom felt great guilt over not fighting for me and marrying me. The guilt he carried was so much like the guilt I felt about not helping my brothers.

Over the course of the evening I learned about Tom's painful marriages, his life, his joys, and his sorrows. I shared what the last nine months had been like for me in my journey to peace. I told him how angry I had been with him for opening up all my old wounds. "What right did you have to do that?" I asked. It was not my idea to make peace with my past and now my life was in turmoil.

He held my hand, looked into my eyes, and repeated to me what he had said on the phone about listening to God's call to be a healer in the world. "I've kept you in my heart all these years and now God had lead me back to you."

"I am the messenger; it's your choice to listen to God's call to heal. I love you enough to tell you the truth." There it was again — a Divine plan. I wasn't alone in thinking that my life had been — and still was — guided by God. Was there really a divine plan unfolding? There are not many people in life who will make us face the stuff we want to forget or push us to heal our wounds. That was the truth he was talking about. He was willing to do that for me even though it made me angry and resentful toward him.

Tom was interested to hear what my life had been like and how I had coped all these years. I explained to him how proficient I'd become at hiding my past, and that I was driven to make my life different than the life I grew up in. I explained to him how I had strived everyday to prove that I was good enough and smart enough. I told him how hard I worked to prove I was worthy of people's love and I had become a workaholic to hide my fear. Fear had always been the main motivator in my life, I explained to him. Fear of not being good enough had served me well, but now I was finally learning to do things out of love for others and myself.

When we finally said goodbye, Tom made one last plea for me to consider friendship. He really wanted to meet my husband and close friends, but I was not comfortable bringing him into my life and family. I didn't think my family would be comfortable with it either. We hugged good-bye, thinking this was probably the last time we would ever see each other.

Though understanding of my need to see Tom, I suspected

that Jerry was worried that he could lose me and that this situation might tear apart our family. He was relieved that I had come home from the meeting with greater understanding, and more importantly, that our marriage was still a priority.

It took me weeks to process everything Tom and I had talked about. Many of my questions had been answered and I gained new insights.

I understood Tom's guilt and regret. I heard about his greatest joys and deepest sorrows. However, he was living in the past; I prayed he would be able to move on. Our meeting gave me the closure I was seeking, leaving no room for re-establishing the friendship he desperately wanted.

I had confided in Betsy and Jane a few months into my struggles. They were the first of my friends that I told. They convinced me that there were many other friends who cared about and wanted to support me. With their help, I started to tell the rest of my friends what was going on with me. This was the first step toward letting people close enough to see the tender places in my heart. I told my friends the truth and they were not judgmental, as I had feared they would be. They were kind and understanding. They remained supportive in the following months and to this day. It felt so wonderful to have what I had been hiding out in the open. Without the support of my close friends I would have never been able to continue in this journey. I could call on them whenever I needed support or reassurance, and I discovered that they were there for me. Always.

Chapter 14

One day after Sunday worship services, Pastor Will took me aside and asked if I would consider working for the church as Director of Shared Ministry which would involve implementing and supporting the church's volunteer programs.

For the last 10 years I had been an avid church volunteer and was in charge of many of the large volunteer projects. My ability to create enthusiasm for projects and carry them out was well-known and respected by the congregation, which is why Will had asked me to consider this job. The job was appealing to me; I could manage volunteer programs with my eyes closed.

Pastor Will knew that I loved my job working with special education kids at school. I was working with kids who came from compromised home situations like I'd come from. It was my calling. My job at school was also secure; the teachers requested that I be in their rooms, it provided great benefits, and I was paid well. Plus I had every summer off as well as the days kids were off school. It was an almost perfect job. I loved it.

Will asked me to strongly consider applying for the church job rather than giving it a flat-out no which I agreed to do. The church position was very tempting but after several weeks of weighing my options I e-mailed Will and told him that, honored as I was to be asked, I had to decline.

Several people at church heard that I turned down the offer and waged a campaign of their own to convince me that this was indeed "my job." It was not only their persistence, but also a gnawing feeling inside me, that made me reconsider. It seems I was not done with this decision yet.

My new experiences dealing with my past were about learning to listen and trust the calling of my heart. My job decision had been made by my head and not from my heart. I asked myself, "What would make me take a cut in pay and lose my benefits, including the insurance that paid for Muriel, to take a job where I would have to work harder and have fewer benefits?" On paper it did not make sense, but my heart was loudly telling me the church job was the right choice. My instincts were too strong to ignore.

Will and the rest of the church staff were elated when I told them my new decision, and I was hired that afternoon. Though I'd accepted the job I still wasn't self-aware enough to understand why, except that it must have been a call from God. Was it there again…a Divine plan?

It took me several months to finish my commitment at

school and to fully transition to the church job. By June I was at church full-time. At the very first staff meeting I attended, there was a guest speaker representing Lutheran Social Services. He was there to ask our church to participate in a partnership with Lutheran Social Services in a new project being developed. The project required a large annual financial contribution from the church as well as a large volunteer commitment. The project was Rezek House, a home for young people aged 16 and 21 who came from from violent homes. I almost fell out of my chair. Was this why I was there? Tears welled up in my eyes and I wondered if I would be able to get through the meeting.

After the meeting Will spoke to me. If the church council approved it, this project would fall under your job responsibilities. "This project is too important not to do," said Will. He would do his best to get the council to understand its significance. I was forced with a big decision I would have to make: Would I keep quiet or would I be open about my childhood?

The council approved only a small portion of the Rezek House project and Will was disappointed. "You and I both know that this isn't good enough," Pastor Will lamented. "It's not what we're capable of doing as a congregation." His next question brought about another major turning point in my healing journey: "Would you tell your story to the church council?" I had just begun sharing my story with a few close friends but I knew this was the next step in my healing process. I had to help our church council grasp the importance of helping children who come from abusive situations. They needed to see that we could make a difference in children's lives. Of course there was only one answer to Will's question, and it was "yes."

At the church council's next meeting I nervously stood before them and told them the story of my life. When I finished the group sat silent, some had tears in their eyes, hardly believing what they heard. They too knew this would be an important outreach project for our church. They approved the project unanimously and enthusiastically, at the same time expressing great sadness over my experiences. Now we had to move on to the next task: create support throughout the congregation.

Telling my story to the council turned out to be just a small step. One day Pastor Will came over to my desk and quietly asked, "Will you share your story at a church service?" I had no idea if I could, but it seemed like another necessary step in my journey towards wholeness that continued to unfold before me.

Before I could share my story with my church congregation, I would have to share it with my family. They'd known something was wrong for many months, but were too afraid to ask what it was. Later I learned that they thought I had cancer or some other terrible illness. I regretted what I had put them through; I loved them very much and hadn't meant to hurt them.

My sons Brent, Chris and Matt were 20, 17 and 13 then. Because they were at different levels of maturity, I talked to them each separately. I told them about my childhood and tried to help them understand the issues I was wrestling with now. I was concerned, rightfully, that they would struggle to understand this difficult information and my pain.

All three boys were very angry with my parents. Neither one of them had shown much interest in being grandparents; therefore my sons only had a limited relationship with them. I hoped I would eventually be able to help my sons work through their questions and anger. At least they finally had answers to what had been wrong with their mom.

Telling my husband was even more complicated. We had never communicated very well. We talked about family and kid issues but never about "us." Throughout our marriage we had passively gone with the flow of things. Our relationship had become routine, a little tired, but secure and comfortable. Jerry had gotten used to my mysterious baggage and it was never discussed. Many times I incorrectly interpreted this as meaning he didn't care about me or what I'd been through (even though he didn't know exactly what it was). Jerry was in a difficult position; if the roles were reversed how would I respond? There was much work to do in our family. Together I hoped we could weather this storm.

On January 21, 2001 I shared my story in front of my church. The night before, I called my friend Jane in a panic. I was hysterical. Why did she let me agree to something so crazy? Surely this was one of the stupidest things I had ever agreed to do. The panic was overtaking me and I couldn't think straight.

"Remember why you agreed to do this?" Jane asked calmly.

I took a few deep breaths and began to relax. I remembered exactly why I was doing this: to bring awareness and compassion for children who come from abusive homes. Compassion comes from understanding. Understanding comes from awareness. I wanted to make people aware that abuse is all around us if we choose to open our eyes, see it and, most importantly, step in and do something about it. It was essential for me to stand up and let people know that every one of us has the opportunity to make a difference in a child's life. This might mean changing our own attitudes about abused children or changing our attitudes about the people who abuse them. The responsibility belongs to all of us to care for all of society's children.

When I spoke that Sunday, I could feel God's presence inside of me as I stood at the pulpit. At first I struggled with the words, but as I continued, I was overtaken by their power. Those words represented the truth of what happened to me, and the truth of who I am. I had been given a gift: the ability to talk about the abuse my brothers and I suffered in a way that could help other people. The Divine plan continued to unfold.

My friends and family, including my brothers, were there to support me that day. It was an important day for all us. I still had much work to do but my life was moving forward in a way I had never envisioned. After I gave this initial speech I went on to speak at many other churches and became a spokesperson for the Rezek House program. Lutheran Social Services asked me to speak at many events including the dedication of Rezek House, which was an enormous honor. I was living my intention. If one person found hope and inspiration in what I said, I will have fulfilled my purpose.

Chapter 15

Even in the midst of the rough times of therapy I felt a growing sense of peace. I could feel it in every part of my body; I felt lighter. As I finally unloaded the truth about what had happened to me I gained insight about who I was. With that came love and compassion for myself. Muriel was teaching me how to love myself. I didn't have to love myself *because* of what happened, but I did need to love myself *despite* what happened.

I was finally beginning to understand what it really meant to heal the body, mind and spirit. In the past I had dealt with problems or situations from a very conscious and logical perspective. I would assess the situation as a whole and decide what needed to be done first and in order. It was all very regimented and controlled; there was a beginning, middle and end. This didn't always work perfectly, but it usually worked well enough to get me by.

But this way of dealing with problems only scratches the

surface, and doesn't get to the root of the problem, so it never really fixes anything. It's covering a wart with a Band-Aid. You may no longer see the wart, but it's still there. True healing doesn't work this way. Things don't heal in a logical, conscious way.

Anger, grief and loss, and forgiveness don't occur in an orderly fashion and they can't be completed as separate tasks. Like a rope is made up of many fibers that are twisted together, my emotions were intertwined. They couldn't be disconnected. There were not predetermined stages to my therapy and healing process. I didn't work on anger first, grief and loss second, and then expect forgiveness at the end.

I was skeptical at first, believing it was all just a coincidence, one thing totally unrelated to the others. Once again my use of logic fell short. There was indeed something else at work here. The hand of God was weaving in and out of my every thought and feeling, helping me recognize what I was being called to do.

Allowing my journey to unfold as it needed to required trust on my part. I already had confirmation that peace was possible. God's plan had led me to Tom's call, which led to my healing, which led to my job change, which led to the Rezek House project and my calling to help others who had endured abusive childhoods.

This is how the rest of this journey to peace would unfold. My anger, my grief and loss, and in the end, the hoped-for forgiveness, would not occur in a logical and predetermined way. And the paths to get there would take on a variety of forms:

talking, guided visualizations, hypnosis, Reiki, and other experiences. Allowing me to access my unconscious and spiritual realms of my mind would be essential to my healing.

My first task was simply to acknowledge my feelings without judging them as good or bad, I just had to be present with the experience. To help myself I picked up books on spirituality. When Muriel would talk about some aspect of spirituality in our session I would go home and read everything I could about it. Forgiveness was the first place I started, reading many different authors with many points of view. I had to understand as much as I could and then weigh it against my own criteria. I would sit with it, question it, and then — and only then — if it fit for me, I would make it my own.

The very first thing that Muriel taught me was that forgiveness is something one does for oneself so one can move on. It means finding forgiveness within yourself without having to involve the other person. It was clear to me that my dad would never acknowledge what he had done or apologize for it. Forgiveness did not mean that what he did was right, nor did it mean we would have to have a relationship. This was different than what I had always believed, but thanks to Muriel and much reading, I was able to change my perspective on this.

We can make up our minds that we will forgive someone, but it is very different to actually *feel* that forgiveness. Real transformation takes place when we live our lives according to what we believe.

Meditation and journaling has become a spiritual practice for me. My usual ritual is to find a comfortable place to sit where I will not be disturbed. To signal the beginning of this sacred time I light a candle or play my Tibetan singing bowl. The bowl is made from seven different metals. I play it with a wooden mallet which glides it around the rim, causing it to sing. It is used to signal a beginning and ending time to prayer or meditation. With my eyes closed I concentrate on each breath, breathing deeply and exhaling slowly. I continue to do this until my breathing became effortless. In my mind I can visualize the circular motion of my breath. If my conscious mind starts to wander I bring my attention back and allow myself access to the unconscious part of my mind.

During my time of meditation and visualization, I would often come to a new awareness about something or a solution to a problem would become clear. Sometimes I heard God talking to me — guiding me where I needed to go. I usually ended this time by setting an intention for the day and saying prayers.

Many days I would write about whatever was on my mind. Journaling made it easier for me to clarify an issue and then let it go. Sometimes, as a "letting go" ritual, I burned what I had written because it represented something that was no longer useful to me. Many times I couldn't resolve a problem until I had written it down.

My intention wasn't always to solve a problem. Sometimes it was to feel compassion for others, to open my heart to love, or to let go of the need to be right or to not judge others. Meditation and journaling helped me to embrace all that life had to offer. They guided my days and made me aware of my feelings. Working on what came up in meditation or journaling allowed me to know what needed attention next. By setting intentions I would look for ways they were true and somehow I portrayed a more positive energy. The world seemed to align with that energy and helped my intentions happen.

Each day as I awoke I would greet the day with awe and reverence for the opportunity to create a new experience. Meditation and journaling were a commitment I made to my healing and myself, and are practices I still use. My day still starts with meditation. It's become a way to help me focus on what's important and allows me to listen to my heart. I had become a master at ignoring my own needs but meditation lets me honor those needs.

When life gets in the way of this process (which sometimes happens for days and even weeks) I'll find myself caught in a negative cycle that's hard to get out of. A friend once told me "you always struggle when you abandon yourself." She was absolutely right.

Our values and beliefs are part of our unconscious mind. Everything that we do is based on a value or belief, whether we recognize it as such or not. If we want to change a behavior we have to first understand its underlying value or belief. Sometimes our actions are based on values that were instilled in us as children. The action may no longer serve us, and may actually be the cause of the problem, but we're not aware of its deeper source. Once we understand this, we're in a position to heal the old hurts and change our actions to reflect our new beliefs and values. In my case, not communicating well with my husband was an action I wanted to change. It was based on my long-held belief that opening up would only bring me heartache.

The inner work I was doing was beginning to show on the outside. I felt like I had more control of my life, and I was becoming more at peace myself. Muriel was teaching me how to focus on what was on the inside. She used guided visualizations to help me see my heart open and allow love to flow through it and penetrate my being. I was learning to listen for and trust the voice that was inside of me that whispered in my heart.

It had always been easy for me to be analytical about what had happened. Now I was aware that what made sense in my head often conflicted with what I felt in my heart. Each of us has available to us three different realms of our minds: the conscious, the unconscious, and the spiritual. With Muriel's guidance, I was now learning to access the spiritual and unconscious realms. In the coming months they would become an essential part of my journey to heal.

As time went by I became more and more aware that Grandma Selma was right; our lives are journeys with lessons to be learned and blessings to be acknowledged. One big lesson for me has been learning to trust in a power greater than myself.

Another is understanding that we are all one with each other and the universe. Our lives are part of a sacred plan, the purpose unfolding as our journey continues. Along the way we have many choices to make. These choices are what make up our lives. Our challenge is to discern for ourselves if our choices will be guided by fear or love. I was forced to learn early that fear and love cannot coexist together. Then I discovered that fear will give way to love if we allow ourselves to feel unconditional love for others and accept it for ourselves. When we open ourselves up in this way we discover that we are an expression of the love God has shown us.

Chapter 16

"It's hard to dance with the devil on your back." These words from an old folk song were filled with meaning for me as I struggled through my present circumstances. The more work I did, the more I realized how much anger I was carrying that I wasn't consciously aware of. It *was* hard to dance with this devil inside of me. I was angry about my whole childhood for everything that did and didn't happen.

I was angry with my dad for the way he treated my brothers and me. For a while I even hated him.

I was angry with my mom for not protecting us.

I was mad at society for not helping us

I was mad at God for not taking care of us

I was mad at Bud for raping me.

I was mad about not having a true childhood.

My anger had to be brought into the open so I could be let it go. After years of being pushed down, it was buried deeply. Digging it out was going to be ugly and uncomfortable.

When my anger finally came out it took many forms. Sometimes I would find a private place to yell and scream. Sometimes, I am ashamed to admit, my family would bear the brunt of it. Many times it sneaked up on me at the most inappropriate times, and I would confuse it with something else. I wrote letters to my dad and to Bud. I never intended to send them but this exercise allowed me a way to express how angry I felt about what they had done. It felt good to let go of the negative energy.

Muriel guided me inside myself and had me separate myself from my dad and Bud. I visualized them a safe distance from me and I told them all the hurt they had inflicted. I told my dad how much it hurt when he beat me, how scared I was all the time for our safety. I told him how worthless he made me feel, how I desperately wanted him to love me, and how all I had wanted was to be his little girl.

I told Bud what it felt like to be raped over and over again, how he deceived me by not giving me the safe home he'd promised, how he stole something from me that I could never get back.

All of the feelings and emotions that were present when these terrible events first occurred came out of me. I could actually feel the poison that was inside of me leave my body.

Reiki was another method I used to rid myself of the huge amount of negative energy I carried. Reiki is a type of energy work similar to healing touch. Our bodies have seven energy centers, called chakras that correspond to specific emotions. The Reiki practitioner gently puts his/her hands on or above one of the energy centers. The energy of the universe comes through the practitioner, into the person receiving it, and then flow back out to the universe.

This practice allows the body to access its own healing power and balance the energy within the body. Through this touch we give and receive love at the same time. What a nice harmony to both give and receive the love the universe has to offer. My first Reiki experience was the first time I had ever allowed anyone to touch me with love without sexual connotations. It was an overpowering experience. Could I really deserve this love? I felt so safe letting down all my defenses and feeling my own pain. In the process of letting go I could feel the energy that filled the room. My heart opened and I could feel myself absorb all the love that the universe had to offer. I felt a connection to everyone and everything. This made sense because, after all, we're all connected. I'd never had an experience like this before; even amidst my utter exhaustion, I felt peace and love and knew that I wasn't alone in the room that day. Sent to support me, Angels and guides, surrounded me. No words that exist can describe the power of my experience.

Since the beginning of this journey I have sought peace.

There is a law of opposites: If we have anger, we can't have peace. If we have hate we cannot have love. It was time to let my anger go. Little by little as I learned how to find peace in my heart, I also found compassion. I could visualize my heart opening to the love of others and the love of God. When I think about the world and all the violence in it, I wonder how we can find peace in our world if we cannot first find it in our own hearts.

One day I arrived at Muriel's office very angry. She made me sit down at her desk and write about my anger. She instructed me to keep the pen to the paper and keep writing. Finally, in anger and exasperation I screamed "don't you ever get tired of this?"

She replied, "Do you mean do I ever get tired of helping people learn to love themselves? No, I never get tired of that!" With those words, my anger turned to tears and I remembered that love heals everything.

Once I could look beyond his behavior, I was able to see that my dad was not born with a hateful heart. Like all of us, he was created in God's image. Until they are taught to hate, children only know how to love. My dad had been badly wounded too. Could I hold him responsible for what was done to him? He behaved the only way he knew how. Now I could make a choice to hold onto my hate and anger or stop the cycle and learn to love him despite his hateful ways.

If this was true for my dad was it not true for my mom as well? My mother had been mentally ill all of her life. She was unable to care for herself, much less her children. Muriel suggested to me that my mom and dad were exactly the same except that dad expressed his anger outwardly and mom held hers inside. They both carried anger that could not be penetrated by love.

My mother simply wasn't available emotionally or physically. But like any child, I had wanted and needed a mom. I wanted her to wipe away my tears and brush her fingers through my hair, the way moms are supposed to do. But I could not get back what was lost or the innocence that went with it. What I *could* do was acknowledge my grief and anger in order to let it go so I could move on. When I learned to let go of the anger, loss and hurt, forgiveness could start.

These therapy sessions were exhausting but, encircled by my angels and guides to help me, I knew I wasn't in it alone. Sometimes Muriel and I simply felt their comforting presence and other times we asked for their guidance and healing.

On days when my work had been especially difficult I had an overwhelming sense that Grandma Selma's spirit was right next to me. I was certain that Grandma was there.

One night I had a dream that grandma "met" Muriel. Grandma had always wanted to meet my friends. This was her way of making sure I had "good" people in my life. In my dream she called Muriel, introduced herself and asked if Muriel would mind making the hour-long drive to her house. (Grandma never got her driver's license.) I saw Muriel pull up in the driveway, clearly picturing grandma's green rambler with white trim. As if I were a fly on the wall, I saw the two of them sitting at the kitchen table drinking coffee and eating sweets. The kitchen table was where all of grandma's serious conversations took place. They made small talk and then grandma leaned closer to Muriel, about to launch into the important part of their meeting…and I woke up.

I had once asked Muriel if she could feel Grandma Selma in the room with us. When I told Muriel about the dream her response was "Let's ask grandma about it." I refused, unwilling to do this "uncovery" work myself, but Muriel pressed on. She was particularly tough on me that day, much harder on me than usual; I almost walked out. Her intent was to make me take responsibility for my healing, which I thought I'd been doing. In truth I was playing the victim, which was easier, and less scary, than moving forward.

Grandma never allowed anyone to stay a victim for long. I think that we both felt her presence with us that day, pushing me to do the hard work. In life Grandma Selma was always hard on me; she believed that I would only learn life's lessons if she pushed me. There's no doubt that Grandma's wisdom and teaching was being channeled through Muriel.

Grandma Selma's voice also came through in both my meditation and my dreams. I have very vivid dreams that play out various aspects of my life. For 10 years I had a reoccurring dream that I had lost something very important to me and I would wake up in a panic. You don't have to be Sherlock Holmes to figure out that it was I who was lost. That dream ended while I was working with Muriel and has never returned. When meditating I continue to ask for Grandma Selma's guidance when needed.

Sometimes events would occur in my dreams before they actually happened in real life. It was sobering to realize that an event that had just happened actually came to me in a dream first. Many times the dreams had important messages for me to consider. These dreams would often bring clarity to issues I had been working on for a long time. Through this I learned to pay attention to, and trust, my intuition.

On several occasions I've visited the sites where my abuse took place, sometimes friends came with me to offer support and sometimes I went alone. It has never been clear to me what called me back to those places. One day after a session in which we'd made great progress, Muriel suggested we go back to these places together.

We left one morning in a pouring rainstorm. With each mile we drove the sky became clearer and the rained stopped. We drove to the first place I had lived, the house by the South Center Lake in Lindstrom, Minnesota and parked the car. I sat in silence remembering all the drama that occurred there and thinking about all I had learned over the last several months. This time I was there to acknowledge my experience, forgive the past, let it go, and bless what lay ahead.

We followed the road around the lake, the same road I had walked so often as a girl. We lit a candle at the same place where I used to sit when I went down to the lake. There we sat in silence, admiring the magnificence of nature as I silently forgave and blessed my past. I savored all the learning I had done and the wisdom that I was taking into my future. Muriel and I walked down to the waters edge and knelt beside the water. I scooped up a handful of sand and imaged it was all the hurt I'd felt. As I let the sand fall through my fingers to be carried away in the water, I offered a prayer and a blessing to all of life.

Our next destination was the second place my family had lived, just a few miles from this house. The old house was gone and had been replaced by a new one, but I could still feel the painful memories there. As we parked on the side of the road, three beautiful horses came out of the pasture and walked right up to the fence. They looked at us as though they had something to say. The ache of my past seemed to dissipate and now, in this peaceful and serene setting, I could see my three brothers, strong and healthy despite our childhoods.

We moved on to the cafe where I had lived and worked. Bud and Rose were long gone. I had heard that they had retired and moved to a neighboring town. The restaurant was vacant but it looked as though someone was living upstairs. As we sat in front I was overcome with emotion. Muriel took out a Bible and began to read the 21st Psalm.

I got out of the car, and walked up to the building, and

peered into the restaurant, picturing the young girl who once lived, worked, and was harmed there. I tried the door; it was open and I walked inside. As I did so, all the hurt and anguish of what had happened there broke through the surface and poured out of me.

I wasn't aware that Muriel was beside me until she wiped the tears from my face. She started to sing. "Dona Nobis Pacem, Pacem. Dona Nobis Pacem." Grant us peace. We stood in that space together, letting peace wash over us and through us. I had never felt this kind of peace before; it was glorious and intoxicating.

The therapeutic work I was doing and the spiritual practices that accompanied it were becoming an integral part of me. I was finally finding balance in my life. As a result of letting go of what no longer served me I was able to pay attention to what really matters. My anger had given way to harmony and love. I was able to let go of so many of the judgments I'd made about others and myself.

I began living each day with intention and purpose, secure in the knowledge that life only offers us the experiences and lessons we need. We are part of each other's lives through a force much bigger than any of us can ever imagine.

My inner transformation radiated outward to my family. We were becoming more harmonious and open to conversation, which enhanced our relationships, and bridged the gap between us.

Chapter 17

I've learned the hard way that healing is ongoing, not a single event. When I think about this now I realize how naive I was for most of my life. I didn't understand anything at all about transformation. I thought that therapy was a magic potion and once the "abracadabras" were said, it would be over and my life would be pretty much the same as it had been. I had no interest in being at the mercy of my past; as far as I was concerned I would prefer it never reared its ugly head again.

At some level I understood that change was inevitable, I just didn't know how profound that change would be and how much it would continue to affect every part of me. Who knew that it was impossible to undo what I'd learned? Lessons once learned are always available to us. One of the numerous things I'd discovered about myself was what triggered certain responses in me.

Once I was aware of a cycle when I was stuck, I could rid

myself of the behaviors that triggered it by choosing to respond in a way that was positive and helped me move past them.

Getting stuck in a victim mode is something that happened to me quite often. Usually it would be triggered by an incident or something someone said to me. Quickly I would revert back to old patterns that were negative and self-destructive. They were always accompanied with statements that validated how unworthy and how unlovable I thought I was. I don't get stuck in this as much as I used to but sometimes it sneaks up on me before I even recognize it, making me stop to resolve it. In the past, I did not have any understanding of myself so I could not change it, letting it build and build, until it was intolerable.

This process is never easy, but the more you are aware of yourself, the easier it becomes to address the issue before it builds. The more emotion that is attached to a behavior, the harder it is to work through. Understanding what your emotion is about leaves you at choice to change it. Sometimes it feels as though no progress has been made at all because emotion has overshadowed the learning. Once the emotion is dealt with the learning can be recognized

Healing is never fully complete. If we are open to it, all our life experiences show us what needs healing. This was especially apparent to me near the end of my therapy. Life was beginning to feel almost normal. I was excited and energized each day and I no longer felt hopeless. Our family was doing well and for the first time in a long time I looked — and felt — happy.

Arriving home late one afternoon I found my husband waiting with unexpected news: My dad had died that afternoon. I was shocked. He'd had virtually no health problems and had not been sick. We later learned that he probably had had a heart attack. My first words were "I thought I had more time."

I had finally arrived at a place of forgiveness for him, though I hadn't spoken to him for the last year because I was still working out my feelings. During that year he had not contacted me either. Now it felt like all the issues I had worked so hard to unravel were once again tied up in knots. My heart felt as heavy as when this ordeal started.

The timing of his death was interesting. I'd been doing a lot of public speaking about my life and child abuse. Dad's death was in mid-October; in November an article I'd written was being published in "The Family Support Networker," a publication of Prevent Child Abuse America. Though I didn't think he would see the article, I thought he might hear about it from someone. Since I had started speaking in public about the abuse, I was constantly terrified he would find out and confront me about what I was saying. Once I dreamt that during a speech I saw him sitting in the front row of the audience and woke up in a panic.

In the days following our father's death, my brothers and I talked at length about our childhood. The evening of his death we went to his home. After I left my brothers remained behind with dad's wife, Eleanor. Royce told her what our lives had been like. My brothers told her why our relationships had been so strained and why we were so distant from him. Then she solemnly explained that our dad had never understood why we acted the way we did toward him until the past year when he finally understood all the harm he had done. I still have no idea what could have been the catalyst for that change of heart.

We cannot always heal our lives in our lifetimes. I believe this was certainly true for my dad. I believe that over the last year he was aware — if not consciously, then unconsciously — that I was addressing the pain that he had caused.

From my first sessions with Muriel, I knew that I would never talk to him about what he had done. He had no intention of saying he was sorry and according to conversations Royce had had with him, he had obviously blocked out the worst of what he had done. Since he didn't have the awareness he needed to find peace here, he would have to work through it in heaven.

I also knew that one day I would get a visit from his spirit and I was terrified of not knowing when. It happened about a year after he died while I was on a horseback riding retreat in Montana.

On one of the first days out, we were riding on trails among 100-year-old trees in the serene and beautiful forest. As I rode I heard a voice inside me that told me why my dad had been the man he was. The voice explained that he couldn't help his violent behavior. He'd provided horses for my brothers and me when we were kids because he understood their healing powers. He knew of the bond we would form with them that would help us cope with our chaotic lives. All of us still love to ride horses and my brothers have several horses of their own.

At first I was sure that the voice I was hearing was my own, though I was surprised by the wisdom I was imparting upon myself. Hours later as I processed the information I knew undeniably that the voice had indeed been my dad's. A sense of panic overcame me and I left the group I was having dinner with, went outside and started to run. I ran on and on... through the ranch, down the road and into the pasture. I ran until my legs gave out, just like I had the day that dad had tried to kill us. But as hard and far as I'd run this time, there was no running away; dad was making his peace with me whether I liked it or not. I could choose to embrace it or keep running. Since I had already forgiven him, I was willing to let go and let there be peace between us.

But I wasn't prepared for his death. I felt like I was back at square one, but I wasn't. I didn't slip back to the terrible place I had started. It was a step back, but I now had within me all the learning that had taken place that I could access. In some ways it was a more difficult place to be than where I had first started because now I was forced to make use of everything I had learned and was aware of the consequences if I didn't.

A few weeks before my dad died Muriel and I had ended our therapeutic relationship. After he died, I thought that this may not have been the best idea. How could I go on without her help? She obviously didn't care about me as much as I had thought or she would continue to help me through this.

Feeling alone and afraid, I went to her and implored her to continue our therapy. "No, you don't need a therapist," she replied. She was as sure of this as she was sure of the fact that I didn't know it. It was time for me to use the skills I had learned "without a net." She'd taught me how to be present with my pain and deal with it. No one else can heal my pain for me. I knew how to take responsibility for what I feel, love it and let it go. I had learned that doing so has the capacity to transform my life; my dad's death would again transform me, just like every experience does.

At the end of my very first session with Muriel she had said, "This is the beginning of the journey." What I didn't know then, but am now acutely aware of, is that this journey takes place over the course of our lives. When we are perceptive to what life offers us, life will always show us what needs to be healed.

Many times when we are presented with the opportunity for growth we have a choice to go along willingly or to fight. I had trouble learning that because my fear of feeling always made me fight. After all, my entire childhood had been a fight so it was my natural response. But as I learned to trust myself, I knew I had the tools I needed to cope. I could embrace times of darkness with more ease, knowing that all the resources I needed were within me.

Just a month and a half after my dad died, Tom — the man who had put me on the road to this remarkable journey — died.

He had lung cancer for at least a year, but had not shared this with me during any of our conversations. My suspicion is that he knew he was dying when he first called me that Sunday afternoon. If not, I believe he was aware on an unconscious level that his time was short.

Tom had called me a few weeks before his death. He expressed disappointment that I hadn't allowed him to come and hear me speak about child abuse. He also again said he was sad that I wouldn't let him meet my husband, sons and close friends. I said again that this didn't feel right and was not respectful of my family and friends. He asked me to think about it again and let him know. But it was not meant to be, of that I was certain. He didn't sound like himself, but I didn't know why. Now it's obvious that he was quite sick when he'd called.

Two weeks later I received a call from Tom's sister telling me that he was in hospice care. She told me that, in the presence of his pastor, his wife and herself, he stated that I had been the love of his life and that he wanted me to know that he was dying. I was told that his wife accepted this with exceptional grace. She loved him unconditionally and wanted to grant him his dying wish. She even got a pencil and paper to write down my number, and then asked his sister to call me. Imagine the kind of love this gesture took.

His sister told me that Tom had wanted me to know that he had never stopped loving me. I had never stopped loving Tom either. He and I had an indescribable connection that had been present since we first met. It spanned the years that we were apart. At one time it was a romantic love. We both thought that we would marry and spend our lives together, but that wasn't God's plan. This wasn't something that could be easily understood. How could two people who were so in love not be allowed to spend their lives together?

The recent love I felt for him was for the person he was and the gifts he brought to the world. It was a beautiful kind of love, a love where you're cared for and prayed for even when you haven't talked in 30 years. All those years he'd held my well-being in his heart. I only wish he had not lived a life of regret.

When Tom called me that fateful Sunday afternoon he was still feeling the loss of our relationship and concerned about me making peace with my past. Later as I watched my life unravel, I could see that there was something much bigger at work in my life: the unfolding of something divine. It was clear to me that his role in my life had been to care for my spirit. Every time I forgot he reminded me that he was my healer who had been sent by God to find me.

All the old belief systems on which I based my life were no longer useable. A friend of mine wrote a song that included the line, "There is nothing from my old life that I can hang on to." That is exactly how I felt. I had totally transformed every part of me. Friends said to me, "You are changing so fast we hardly recognize you." I hardly recognized me either. It was difficult to embrace all the changes that were going on inside of me. "I don't know who I am," I said to myself more than once. The truth was that, for the first time, I was getting closer to my authentic self.

Early in my therapy Muriel defined peace as "telling your story without the emotion." What this meant to me was that my peace would be found by changing my relationship to what occurred. What happened will never change, the memories will remain, but I have changed how I view them. Despite Grandma Selma's advice, I would never have said that my memories are blessings to acknowledge, but now I know they are. My life experience will help me to do the kind of work I was meant to do. I have always wanted to help people heal from their pain. How could I do that for others if I had not done it for myself?

This process has taught me to form a union of my head and heart. I have used my head to remember and my heart to understand and both to compassionately forgive and move on.

It took courage to look into the dark places in my past and believe that what I found there would set me free. This courage came from the wisdom that I found within myself. I have lived, breathed and felt the truth in every cell of my body. This is wisdom: using what we have learned, through what we've read, what others have taught us, and our experiences, and then to take all these learnings and apply them to our own circumstances, making them our own.

As I look back at my life I can see the threads of Grandma Selma's wisdom woven through every part of it. Those threads of wisdom helped me create a spiritual foundation that became a catalyst for me to build upon.

Marianne Williamson, a favorite spiritual writer of mine, summarizes my extensive journey in two profound quotations from her writings:

"The woman who can give hope to those who have no reason to hope; the woman who can endure deep pain and know that this shall pass, and can hold on until it does — the woman who can do and say these things, and has the courage to mean them, carries a conviction that makes them true."

"But we can choose to emerge like newborn babies from the womb of our yesterdays. To be born a girl is a gift we were given. To become a real woman of wisdom and courage is a gift we give the world."

As I said before, something always drew me back to the place where the abuse happened. It was as though I was going back there to search for peace. Though we all know now that the peace I sought was already within me, sometimes going back helped me access the insight and wisdom I needed to heal. On that final trip to the lake with Muriel I burned some old letters and pictures of my dad and Bud. They represented things I no longer needed. At the end we offered prayers and I gathered up the ashes from what I had burned. Taking the remains to the lake I allowed them to be swept away in the current of the water. This simple ritual honored the hard work that had been done. We also wanted to acknowledge all that the future represented.

"We have one more thing to do here," Muriel said. She took a ceramic bowl from her car, we went down to the lake and put some water in the bowl. Next to the water, we stood face to face. Muriel dipped her finger in the water gently put her finger to my forehead and said, "You are re-baptized into a new life with Christ" as she made the sign of the cross on me.

I could feel the spirit move in and around us. Muriel poured the remaining water on the ground and stated, "This is hallowed ground." Indeed it was; every step we take is on hallowed ground. When we see God in everything and every one, we see the divine in all of life. Life is extraordinary when we acknowledge this, and see it and feel it for ourselves.

For those of you about to start, or are continuing your journeys, I wish you peace in your mind and your spirit. Trust that you have within yourself everything you need to heal and trust your own heart to love you all along the way.

AUTHOR'S COMMENTS

As I said in the book, I never really thought it was possible to heal from the trauma of my childhood. That is why I wanted this book to include my journey to wholeness, as well as the telling of the story. It would be incomplete to tell one without the other. You see, they are two sides of the same coin.

I am still that needy, vulnerable child that is portrayed in parts of the book. I find that when I abandon myself by not listening and honoring my deepest knowing, I can fall victim to fear and self-doubt. From this perspective, I become my own worst enemy, allowing myself to be stuck in a downward spiral. Stuck in my past, I am unable to move forward into my dreams and aspirations.

If I am quick to tell you what is undesirable about me, I also need to embrace what my attributes are. This is harder for me to do, as it is for many of us. However, this is the other side of the coin. So as well as being vulnerable, I can also be courageous and fearless, embracing my life with love and compassion.

Coming into who we are, is dependent upon embracing all that is desirable as well what is undesirable. When we acknowledge what no longer works we are in a position to change it. Through this process I learned to tell the truth about my life, forgive myself and others, and let go of limiting beliefs. I found the spirit of the creator that resides in my own heart and I could nurture it with compassion and love. I have learned that love is truly the only healer. First, unconditional love for yourself and then allowing that love to flow through you and out into the world.

It is from this perspective that I wanted to help other's find peace and possibility in their life; in fact it is my passion. In my coaching practice it is my mission to help people tell the truth about their lives, transform their pain, nurture their spirit and attain the dreams they desire. Through speaking engagements and workshops I teach people tools that they can use to change their own life.

It is also my passion to help bring about awareness of child abuse so we can all chose to be part of the solution. Sometimes that is as simple as offering a prayer on behalf of vulnerable children. I often speak at conferences on vulnerable children helping professionals understand what it is like to be an abused child. It is from this place of understanding that a professional can create and nurture a life-affirming relationship with a child. The most common comment I hear from professionals is, "I will never look at the child I am working with the same way again after hearing your story." That makes it all worth it.

And so if one person finds hope and inspiration in reading this book, it is indeed worth it. My prayer for you is that your life is touched by love often and that you nurture the spirit of God that is inside your soul, acknowledging all the blessings of life.

Namaste,

Sandy

Reflections